FASCISM VIEWED FROM THE RIGHT

Original: *Il fascismo visto dalla destra; Note sul terzo Reich*,
Rome: G. Volpe, 1974.

First English edition published in 2013 by Arktos Media Ltd.

Published in the United Kingdom.

ISBN **978-1-907166-85-3**

BIC classification:
Social & political philosophy (HPS)
Fascism & Nazism (JPFQ)
Nationalism (JPFN)

Translation: E. Christian Kopff
Editor: John B. Morgan
Cover Design: Andreas Nilsson
Layout: Daniel Friberg

ARKTOS MEDIA LTD
www.arktos.com

FASCISM VIEWED FROM THE RIGHT

BY JULIUS EVOLA

Translated with an Introduction by E. Christian Kopff

ARKTOS
LONDON 2013

A Note from the Editor

The footnotes to the Introduction were added by E. Christian Kopff. The footnotes to the text itself were added by me. The second Italian edition of this work contained a number of footnotes added by Evola himself. To avoid confusion, these have been included as part of the main body of the text, but are bracketed and indicated to make it clear that they are notes.

Where sources in other languages have been cited, I have attempted to replace them with existing English-language editions. Citations to works for which I could locate no translation are retained in their original language. Web site addresses for on-line sources were verified as accurate and available during December 2012.

I would like to thank Professor E. Christian Kopff for his work on this volume and for his dedication to ensuring that it has been held to the highest quality standards possible. This book would not have been realised without his extraordinary and generous efforts.

—JOHN B. MORGAN IV

INTRODUCTION

By the early 1960s, Julius Evola (1899-1974) felt he had written his most important books, *Revolt Against the Modern World*,[1] *Men Among the Ruins*[2] and *Ride the Tiger*,[3] and composed *The Path of Cinnabar*[4] as a retrospective on his entire *oeuvre*. He decided to present his views on Italian Fascism, and later on, German National Socialism, the twentieth century political movements he knew best from personal experience. The first work was published in 1964 as *Fascism: Essay of a Critical Analysis from the Point of View of the Right*[5] and reprinted with additional notes in 1970 as *Fascism Viewed from the Right*.[6]

Evola had a variegated career. In his youth, he was the major Italian Dadaist poet and painter (1916-1922). He then became the leading Italian exponent of the intellectually rigorous esotericism of René Guénon (1886-1951). He enjoyed an international reputation for books on magic, alchemy and Eastern religious traditions, winning the respect of such important scholars as Mircea Eliade and Giuseppe Tucci. In his lifetime, only one of his many books, *The Doctrine of Awakening*, a 1943 interpretation of early Buddhism, was published in an English translation (1951).[7] In 1983, Inner Traditions International published *The*

1   *Rivolta contro il mondo moderno* (Milan: Hoepli, 1934); translated as *Revolt Against the Modern World* (Rochester, VT: Inner Traditions, 1995).

2   *Gli uomini e le rovine* (Rome: 1953), revised 1967); translated as *Men Among the Ruins* (Rochester, Vermont: Inner Traditions, 2002).

3   *Cavalcare la tigre* (Milan: All'Insegna del Pesce d'Oro, 1961); translated as *Ride the Tiger* (Rochester, VT: Inner Traditions, 2003).

4   *Il cammino del cinabro* (Milan: All'Insegna del Pesce d'oro, 1963); translated as *The Path of Cinnabar* (London: Arktos Media, 2009).

5   *Il fascismo: saggio di una analisi critica dal punto di vista della destra* (Rome: G. Volpe, 1964).

6   *Il fascismo visto dalla destra; Note sul terzo Reich* (Rome: G. Volpe, 1974).

7   *La dottrina del risveglio* (Bari: G. Laterza & figli, 1943), revised in 1965; translated as *The Doctrine of Awakening* (London: Luzac, 1951).

Metaphysics of Sex (1958),[8] which it reprinted as *Eros and the Mysteries of Love* in 1992, the same year it published his 1949 book on Tantra, *The Yoga of Power.*[9] Since then, English translations of many of his books have been published.[10]

In Europe, Evola is known not only as an esotericist, but also as a brilliant and incisive Right-wing thinker. During the 1980s, his traditionalist and political books were translated into French.[11] His books and articles have been translated into German since the 1930s.[12] Discussion of Evola's politics reached North America more slowly. In the 1980s, the political scientists Thomas Sheehan, Franco Ferraresi and Richard Drake presented him unsympathetically, blaming him for neo-Fascist terrorism.[13] In 1990 the esoteric journal *Gnosis* published articles on Evola by Robin Waterfield and Italian esotericist Elémire Zolla.[14] The essay by *Gnosis* editor Jay Kinney is devoted to Evola's 'Fascism'. He seems not to have read Evola's books in any language, called *The Metaphysics of Sex* Evola's 'only book translated into English' and concluded that 'Evola's esotericism appears to be well outside of the main currents of Western tradition. It remains to be seen whether his Hermetic virtues can be disentangled from his political sins. Meanwhile, he serves as a persuasive argument for the separation of esoteric "Church and State"'.[15]

---

8   *Metafisica del sesso* (Rome: Atanòr, 1958), revised 1968; translated as *The Metaphysics of Sex* (New York: Inner Traditions, 1983).

9   *Lo Yoga della potenza* (Milan, 1949,) revised in 1968 (Rome: Edizioni mediterranee, 1968), new edition of *L'Uomo come Potenza* (Rome: Atanòr, 1926); translated as *The Yoga of Power* (Rochester, VT: Inner Traditions, 1992).

10 *The Path of Cinnabar*, p. ix.

11 Robin Waterfield, 'Baron Julius Evola and the Hermetic Tradition' in *Gnosis* 14 (1989-90), pp. 12-17.

12 Karlheinz Weissman, 'Bibliographie' in *Menschen immitten von Ruinen* (Tübingen: Hohenrain-Verlag, 1991), pp. 403-406.

13 Thomas Sheehan, 'Myth and Violence: The Fascism of Julius Evola and Alain de Benoist', in *Social Research* 48 (1981), pp. 45-73; Franco Ferraresi, 'Julius Evola: Tradition, Reaction and the Radical Right', in *Archives européennes de sociologie* 28 (1987), pp. 107-151; Richard Drake, 'Julius Evola and the Ideological Origins of the Radical Right in Contemporary Italy', in Peter H. Merkl (ed.), *Political Violence and Terror: Motifs and Motivations* (Berkeley: University of California Press, 1986), pp. 61-89; and Richard Drake, *The Revolutionary Mystique and Terrorism in Contemporary Italy* (Bloomington: University of Indiana Press, 1989), pp. 114-134.

14 Robin Waterfield, ibid.; Elémire Zolla, 'The Evolution of Julius Evola's Thought', *Gnosis* 14 (1989-90), pp. 18-20.

15 Jay Kinney, 'Who's Afraid of the Bogeyman? The Phantasm of Esoteric Terrorism', in *Gnosis* 14 (1989-90), pp. 21-24.

Evola was never a member of the Fascist Party, and during the two decades when Mussolini ruled Italy, Evola published critiques of several distinctive Fascist initiatives, including the Concordat with the Vatican, the violence of Fascist toughs (*gli squadristi*) and Fascist rapprochement with National Socialist views of race. His opposition to the Concordat did not convince Mussolini, who was, however, sufficiently impressed by Evola's critique of 'scientific racism' to give his imprimatur to a German translation of one of his books on race, *Synthesis of the Doctrine of Race*.[16] Evola's criticism of the *squadristi* attracted their unwanted attention, until he received the protection of Roberto Farinacci, the Fascist boss of Cremona. He served as editor of the opinion page of Farinacci's newspaper, *Il Regime Fascista*, from 1934 until 1943. The physical harassment stopped, but at the start of the Second World War, when he attempted to resume his commission as an officer in the Italian army that he had received in the Great War, his refusal to fight a duel with a journalist was used as grounds to deny his request.[17]

Evola's originality lay in his thorough and consistent traditionalism, beginning with this book's witty title. Some Italians defended Fascism and all its works and ways from the March on Rome in October 1922 to Mussolini's resignation on 25 July 1943 — *il Ventennio*, or the 'Twenty Years'. Their motto was *Il Duce ha sempre ragione!* (The Duce is always right!). Others, committed Leftists and less committed compromisers, denied any virtue to Italy's government of that time. In *Fascism Viewed from the Right*, Evola points out the absurdity of both positions and proceeds to a critical analysis of Fascism on the basis of the principles he had expounded and advocated in *Revolt Against the Modern World* and other books and pamphlets. Evola is interested in Fascism's principles. He insists that human failings and historical accidents (what Evola refers to as 'the contingent') should not be held against men or movements unless they can be shown to be the consequences of mistaken principles.

Evola seeks the principles of Fascism in Mussolini's major speeches and initiatives, as well as the article on 'The Doctrine of Fascism' in the *Enciclopedia Italiana*. (This last was officially the work of Mussolini, but is usually attributed to the regime's major philosopher and educational reformer, Giovanni Gentile.)[18]

---

16   *Sintesi di dottrina della razza* (Milan: Hoepli, 1941).

17   H. T. Hansen, 'Preface to the American Edition' in *Men Among the Ruins*, p. xiii.

18   A. James Gregor, *Giovanni Gentile: Philosopher of Fascism* (London: Transaction, 2001), pp. 2-3.

Evola finds that Fascism's principles were often good. The regime was sound in principle but failed during the crisis of the Second World War because Italians had been demoralised by two generations of liberal and radical propaganda since the uniting of Italy, *il Risorgimento*. (For the Left, the *Risorgimento* was the expulsion of foreign and papal rule from Italy by an aroused Italian people who were led by great republican radicals like Garibaldi and Mazzini. Conservatives thought that Victor Emmanuel (Vittorio Emanuele), the King of Piedmont, and his politically astute advisor, Cavour, used Garibaldi and Mazzini to overthrow Italy's traditional regimes, which were replaced with Piedmont's bogus — because politically incoherent — constitutional monarchy.)[19]

Evola explains the principles of a true Right. A strong central state creates a nation and its people, not *vice versa*. At the moral and political centre of the best states is a king (*rex*), who may, however — and under Fascism did — choose a leader (*dux*) to administer the state. Strong central leadership does not subvert and, in fact, encourages subsidiarity or federalism, where most decisions and political activity occur at appropriate lower levels. Subsidiarity does not imply democracy, the kingdom or realm of quantity (René Guénon's *Règne de la Quantity*).[20] On the contrary, Fascism established a Chamber of Corporations where the estates, professions and vocations of the land were represented on the basis of importance and achievement, not of pure number.

In a traditional state, the economy is subordinate to the political. Mussolini denied that *homo oeconomicus* existed. Evola does not agree. Unfortunately, in some people the economic dominates the political, ethical and religious. This psychological condition is a mental illness, *la daimonia dell'economia* (demonic possession by the economy).[21] A healthy state is like a healthy human. Free men are unified and coherent individuals who are not dominated by the outside, physical world, but they are also differentiated, with a proper hierarchy of spirit, soul and body within. The state's economic policy should aim at autarchy, supplying its own needs and healthy desires, without depending on free trade with other countries or finance capitalism. Just as a healthy human avoids excessive or unhealthy eating and drinking and exercises appropriately,

---

19 Evola, *Men Among the Ruins*, pp. 187-189.

20 René Guénon, *Le règne de la quantité et les signes des temps* (Paris: Gallimard, 1945); translated as *The Reign of Quantity and the Signs of the Times* (Ghent, NY: Sophia Perennis, 2001).

21 See *Men Among the Ruins*, Chapter 6.

so a healthy nation privileges independence, cooperation and an almost military morale over a purely economic prosperity and consumerism, on the one hand, or a totally controlled centralised economic planning, on the other. Fascism had these goals and aimed at producing this kind of human being when the war cut short its initiatives before they could reach fruition. The courage and resolution of the Italians who supported the Italian Social Republic in northern Italy after 25 July 1943, although its principles were deficient, showed that Fascism was working, but was not given enough time to succeed.

As in *The Path of Cinnabar*,[22] Evola devotes several pages to explaining his views on race in relationship to Fascism. Mussolini's strongest support for Evola came in relation to this subject, which became an issue after Italy's conquest of Ethiopia in 1936. Influenced by Nazi Germany, Italy passed racial laws in 1938. Evola was already writing on racial views consistent with a traditional vision of mankind and in opposition to what he saw as the biological reductionism and materialism of Nazi racial thought. His writings infuriated Guido Landra, editor of the journal *La Difesa della Razza* (Defence of the Race) and other scientific racists, especially Evola's article 'Scientific Racism's Mistake'.[23] Mussolini, however, praised Evola's 1935 essay on 'Race and Culture' and permitted Evola's *Synthesis of the Doctrine of Race* to be translated into German as *Compendium of Fascist Racial Doctrine* to represent the official Fascist position.[24]

Evola accepts the traditional division of man into body, soul and spirit, and argues that there are races of all three. 'While in a "pure blood" horse or cat the biological element constitutes the central one, and therefore racial considerations can be legitimately restricted to it, this is certainly not the case with man, or at least any man worthy of the name. [...] Therefore racial treatment of man cannot stop only at a biological level.'[25] Just as the state creates people and nation, so the spirit shapes the races of body and soul. Evola wrote a history of racial thought from Classical Antiquity to the 1930s, *The Blood Myth: The Genesis of Racism*.[26] He argued that in addition to scientific racism as practiced by

---

22 *The Path of Cinnabar*, pp. 164-179.
23 'L'Equivoco del razzismo scientifico', *Vita Italiana* 30 (September 1942).
24 'Razza e cultura', in *Rassegna Italiana* (1935); *Sintesi di dottrina della razza*; *Grundrisse der faschistischen Rassenlehre* (Berlin: Edwin Runge Verlag, 1943).
25 *Sintesi di dottrina della razza*, p. 35, note 10.
26 *Il mito del sangue: Genesi del razzismo* (Milan: Hoepli, 1937), revised 1942.

Count de Gobineau, Houston Stewart Chamberlain, Alfred Rosenberg and Landra, there was a tradition that appreciated extra- or super-biological elements and whose adherents included Montaigne, Herder, Fichte, Gustave Le Bon and Evola's friend, Ludwig Ferdinand Clauss, a biologist at the University of Berlin.[27]

Evola's critique of the one-party state as still preserving the idea of a government of *partitocrazia*, rule by parties, echoes a common Italian complaint about parties being more important than the citizens they are supposed to represent. This critique has been influential. In Evola's day, the successor to the Fascist Party was called the Italian Social Movement (MSI), not a party. In Italy Leftists still use the word party. The Communist Party of Italy (CPI) has changed its name (twice) and now calls itself the Democratic Party (PD). (From 1993 until 2007, its name was the Democratic Party of the Left, PDS.) Right-wing organisations prefer names like National Alliance, League of the North and even one named after the soccer cheer, Forza Italia! On the other hand, the American poet Ezra Pound, who lived in Italy under Fascism, admired Fascism's one-party state and argued that America had prospered under one-party rule in the first forty years of the nineteenth century. 'Jefferson governed for twenty-four years in a *de facto* one-party condition. Quincy Adams did NOT represent a return to federalism and the one party (Jeffersonian) continued through the twelve years of Jackson-Van Buren.'[28]

Evola approved of the Fascist commitment to economic autarchy on principle, but there were practical consequences, which he may have viewed as 'contingent'. When Mussolini came to power in 1922, Italy had a rich cultural heritage, but financially and politically it was what we today call a 'third world country'. By the 1930s Italy had a European presence. Mussolini saw to the draining of the Pontine Marshes around Rome, which had been a source of malaria since antiquity. ('Italian marshes/ been waiting since Tiberius' time', Pound wrote in *Canto* 38.61.)[29] Farmers worked the recovered land and villages and small towns were constructed there. This and similar projects restored millions of acres of arable land. They were part of Mussolini's 'wars' for the lira, wheat, country life and population that aimed at giving Italy

---

27   Ludwig Ferdinand Clauss, *Rasse und Seele. Eine Einführung in den Sinn der leiblichen Gestalt* (Munich, 1937); *Rasse ist Gestalt* (Munich, 1937).

28   Ezra Pound, *Jefferson and/or Mussolini* (Liverwright: London, 1933), p. 125.

29   *The Cantos of Ezra Pound* (New York: New Directions, 1970), p. 188-189.

greater control over its destiny. The positive effects on national morale surpassed its economic success, which was not, however, insignificant. From 1925 to 1935, grain production grew significantly, and the importing of foreign grain dropped by 75 %. The crushing national debt was renegotiated from short-term to long-term loans. Servicing the domestic debt went from 28 billion lire a year to 6 billion. Evola is scornful of the population campaign, and it is easy to smile at some of its aspects. Military officers, for instance, were encouraged to greet pregnant women with the Fascist salute. On the other hand, encouraging soldiers and civilians to see themselves as part of a common national life is, perhaps, not ridiculous.[30]

There were also public works projects in addition to the rural initiatives. In Rome, subways and new roads to the Coliseum and the Vatican were constructed to ease traffic congestion. (Rome's two subway lines built under Fascism are still the only active ones.) A large sports complex, the Foro Mussolini, was built for the 1940 Olympics (which was cancelled because of the war). It still houses the soccer stadium and the site of the Italian Tennis Open. The train system was electrified and train stations built in the major cities. Not only did 'the trains run on time', but their journey times were reduced significantly. (The travel time from Rome to Syracuse was cut in half.) Again the question of morale was as significant as the measurable results. The Italian people felt that things were happening in areas of their national life where nothing had been accomplished 'since Tiberius' time'.

There was also a cultural side to Fascism. By its restoration of the ancient Roman fasces, Fascism proclaimed Italy's ancient traditions. It sponsored archaeological projects to uncover the Roman past from the republican temples at Largo Argentina in Rome to excavations at Ostia and Libya. The great Ara Pacis of the Emperor Augustus was recovered from beneath the streets of downtown Rome and, following negotiations with the Vatican for parts preserved there, was restored and displayed near the Tiber, where it can still be seen.[31] But it was not only ancient art that Fascism encouraged. There was a national movie industry in Cinecittà outside Rome (which can be reached by the new Metro

---

30   The facts in this and the next three paragraphs come from Nicholas Farrell, *Mussolini: A New Life* (London: Weidenfeld & Nicolson, 2003), e.g., pp. 185-191, 232-235, and 248-251.

31   E. Christian Kopff, 'Italian Fascism and the Roman Empire', in *Classical Bulletin* 76 (2000), pp. 109-115.

system). Writers and artists like Pirandello, D'Annunzio and Marinetti were honoured. Italy's great past was linked to a creative present and future.

Under Mussolini, Italy became a European power. In 1896, the army of Abyssinia (Ethiopia) soundly defeated the Italian army at the Battle of Adowa (Adwa). It was a fair fight between two equally underdeveloped countries. When Italy invaded Ethiopia in 1936, the world protested against the unequal forces confronting one another. This inequality had developed in the years since 1922. Earlier, in 1934, Mussolini had frustrated Hitler's first attempt to conquer Austria.

Evola may have considered these factors to be contingent, but they follow from principles of which he approved. He was less enthusiastic about what was generally considered Mussolini's most impressive domestic achievement, the Concordat between the Catholic Church and the government of Italy signed in 1929, which ended two generations of hostility between the Church and the Kingdom of Italy.

Evola believed that the transcendent was essential for a true revival, but he did not look to the Catholic Church for leadership. In *Men Among the Ruins*, when the official position of the Church was still strongly anti-Communist, he predicted that the Church would move to the Left, and he repeated his analysis in the second edition of 1967.

[A]fter the times of De Maistre, Bonald, Donoso Cortés, and the *Syllabus* have passed, Catholicism has been characterized by political maneuvering [...] Inevitably, the Church's sympathies must gravitate toward a democratic-liberal political system. Moreover, Catholicism had for a long time espoused the theory of "natural right," which hardly agrees with the positive and differentiated right on which a strong and hierarchical State can be built. [...] Militant Catholics like Maritain had revived Bergson's formula according to which "democracy is essentially evangelical"; they tried to demonstrate that the democratic impulse in history appears as a temporal manifestation of the authentic Christian and Catholic spirit [...] By now, the categorical condemnations of modernism and progressivism are a thing of the past. [...] When today's Catholics reject the "medieval residues" of their tradition; when Vatican II and its implementations have pushed for debilitating forms of "bringing things up to date"; when popes uphold the United Nations (a ridiculous hybrid and illegitimate organization) practically as the prefiguration of a future Christian ecumene—this leaves no doubts as to the direction in which the Church is being dragged. All

things considered, Catholicism's capability of providing adequate support for a revolutionary-conservative and traditionalist movement must
be resolutely denied.[32]

His 1967 analysis mentions Vatican II, but Evola's position on the
Catholic Church went back to the 1920s, when, after his early Dadaism,
he was developing a philosophy based on the traditions of India, the Far
East and ancient Rome under the influence of Arturo Reghini (1878-
1946).[33] Reghini introduced Evola to Guénon's ideas on Tradition and
his own thinking on Roman 'pagan imperialism' as an alternative to the
twentieth century's democratic ideals and plutocratic reality. Working
with a leading Fascist ideologue, Giuseppe Bottai (1895-1959), Evola
wrote a series of articles in Bottai's *Critica Fascista* in 1926-27, prais-
ing the Roman Empire as a synthesis of the sacred and the regal, an
aristocratic and hierarchical system under a true leader. Evola rejected
the Catholic Church as a source of religion and morality independent of
the state, because he saw its universalistic claims as compatible with and
tending toward liberal egalitarianism and humanitarianism, despite its
anti-Communist rhetoric.

Evola's articles enjoyed a national *succès de scandale* and he expanded
them into a book, *Imperialismo Pagano* (1928),[34] which provoked
a heated debate involving many Fascists and Catholics, including
Giovanni Battista Montini (1897-1978), who, when Evola published the
second edition of *Men Among the Ruins* in 1967, had become the liberal
Pope Paul VI. Meanwhile, Mussolini was negotiating with Pope Pius
XI (1857-1939) for a reconciliation in which the Church would give its
blessings to his regime in return for protection of its property and official recognition as the religion of Italy. Italy had been united by the
Piedmontese conquest of Papal Rome in 1870 and the Popes had never
recognised the new regime. So Evola wrote in 1928, 'Every Italian and
every Fascist should remember that the King of Italy is still considered
a usurper by the Vatican.'[35] The signing of the Lateran Accords on 11

---

32   *Men Among the Ruins*, pp. 210-211; *Gli uomini e le rovine*, pp. 15-151. 'A ridiculous
     hybrid and illegitimate organization' translates *questa ridicola associazione ibrida
     e bastarda.*

33   On Reghini, see *The Path of Cinnabar*, pp. 78-80. Elémire Zolla gives the essentials
     about Reghini's influence on Evola in his *Gnosis* essay (note 14, above).

34   *Imperialismo Pagano* (Rome: Atanòr, 1928); translated as *Heathen Imperialism*
     (Kemper, France: Thompkins & Cariou, 2007).

35   *Imperialismo Pagano*, p. 40.

February 1929, remedied that situation and ended the debate. Even Reghini and Bottai turned against Evola.[36]

Evola later regretted the tone of his polemic, but he also pointed out that the fact that this debate took place gave the lie direct to extreme assertions about the supposed lack of freedom of speech in Fascist Italy. Evola has been vindicated on the main point. The Catholic Church accepts liberal democracy and even defends it as the only legitimate regime. The University of Notre Dame is not the only Catholic university with a Jacques Maritain Center, but no Catholic university in America has a centre named after Joseph de Maistre, Louis de Bonald or Juan Donoso Cortés. Pope Pius IX was beatified for proclaiming the doctrine of the Immaculate Conception, not for his *Syllabus Errorum*, which denounced the idea of coming to terms with liberalism and modern civilisation.

Those who want to distance Evola from Fascism emphasise the debate over *Heathen Imperialism*. There are anecdotes about Mussolini's fear of Evola, but the documentary evidence points in the opposite direction. Yvon de Begnac's talks with Mussolini, published in 1990, report Mussolini consistently speaking of Evola with respect. Il Duce had the following comments about the debate over *Heathen Imperialism*:

> Despite what is generally thought, I was not at all irritated by Doctor Julius Evola's pronouncements made a few months before the Conciliation on the modification of relations between the Holy See and Italy. Anyhow, Doctor Evola's attitude did not directly concern relations between Italy and the Holy See, but what seemed to him the long-term irreconcilability of the Roman tradition and the Catholic tradition. Since he identified Fascism with the Roman tradition, he had no choice but to reckon as its adversary any historical vision of a universalistic order.[37]

It is clear that Mussolini respected Evola and was interested in his ideas. When he was rescued by Otto Skorzeny in 1943 and brought to Hitler's military headquarters, known as the Wolf's Lair (*Wolfsschanze*), Evola

36 Richard Drake, 'Julius Evola, Radical Fascism, and the Lateran Accords', in *Catholic Historical Review* 74 (1988), pp. 319-403.

37 Yvon de Begnac, *Taccuini Mussoliniani*, Francesco Perfetti (ed.), (Bologna: Il Mulino, 1990), p. 647.

was one of a select group of Italians to be invited there. (Evola's fluency in German may have been one factor in the decision.)

Evola's interest in and involvement in politics has often been a sticking point with religious traditionalists of all stripes. The true world and final goal of a fulfilled spiritual life is the metaphysical, spiritual world that lies beyond the physical, material world. Why was Evola, who was a master of spiritual doctrine, so interested in contemporary politics? For René Guénon, for instance, attaining spiritual fulfilment is a process of passive withdrawal from the chaos of the material world, to escape involvement in the modern world until its final collapse into chaos. Then, and only then, will there be a role for a new *brahmin* caste to restore a Golden Age on the basis of their knowledge of Tradition. Guénon and Evola agreed on many important issues. For Evola, however, active involvement in the world is a viable route to spiritual realisation.[38] The way of the warrior, that of the *kshatriya* caste, is not inferior to the *brahmin*'s. In the best traditional state, the king embodied the traits of both *brahmin* and *kshatriya*, priest and warrior. This much seems clear from Evola's exposition in *Revolt Against the Modern World* (1934), as well as his earlier *Essays on Magical Idealism* (1925).[39] The issue has been confused by the significant chronological difference between the publication of the first editions of *Men Among the Ruins* in 1953 and *Ride the Tiger* in 1961. As Evola's letters show, he wrote *Ride the Tiger* first, and meant them to be understood together. My own comparison of the relation of *Ride the Tiger* to *Men Among the Ruins* is that of Aristotle's *Ethics* to his *Politics*. For both authors, the two works do not contradict, but supplement one another.

Fascism Viewed from the Right is a model of a traditionalism that is not only spiritual and otherworldly, but permeates all aspects of life. Evola's traditionalism was active in meditation and initiation, but also in politics and mountain climbing. His vision of the past he had lived through was committed and principled, but also disinterested, in the original meaning of that word. Such a vision of the past may have been hard to appreciate when the book was first published, but more than two generations removed from the time of Fascism and Mussolini, it should not be too much to expect us to enter into Evola's spirit. We need not

---

38 For a comparison and contrast of Evola and Guénon, see *The Path of Cinnabar*, pp. 7 and 103-104; and Paul Furlong, *Social and Poliltical Thought of Julius Evola* (London: Routledge, 2011), pp. 27 and 41-45.

39 *Saggi sull'Idealismo màgico* (Rome: Atanòr, 1925).

accept every judgment and may vigorously object to some. In the end, Evola's attempt to combine a disinterested commitment to principle with active involvement in the world provides a model of traditionalism that will remain valid.

—E. CHRISTIAN KOPFF

E. Christian Kopff was born in Brooklyn, New York in 1946. He completed his Bachelor's degree *summa cum laude* at Haverford College, and his Ph.D. in Classics at the University of North Carolina at Chapel Hill. He is currently Associate Professor of Classics at the University of Colorado, Boulder, where he has taught since 1973. He has served as Associate Director of the University's Honors Program since 1990 and as Director of its Center for Western Civilization since 2004. He also works with the University of Urbino in Italy on ancient Greek metrics and lyric poetry. He is a Fellow of the American Academy in Rome and has been awarded grants from the National Endowment for the Humanities. He is the author of *The Devil Knows Latin: Why America Needs the Classical Tradition* (ISI Books, 1999), editor of a critical edition of the Greek text of Euripides' *Bacchae* (Teubner, 1982), translator of Josef Pieper, *Tradition: Concept and Claim* (ISI Books, 2008) and has written articles and reviews on scholarly, pedagogical and popular topics. He is also the translator of Guillaume Faye's *Convergence of Catastrophes*, published in 2012 by Arktos.

I

In the pages that will follow we propose to undertake an examination of Fascism from the point of view of the Right. This examination, however, will be limited to Fascism's general aspect and, basically, will take place on the level of principles. To achieve this it is necessary above all to indicate what we understand by Right, even if this task will not be easy, because it is not possible to furnish the general reader with reference points that have a direct relationship with contemporary reality, nor even with more recent Italian history, that is, the history of Italy since it was unified as a nation.

On the first point we must say that there does not exist in Italy today a Right worthy of this name, a Right as a unified political force that is organised and furnished with a precise doctrine. What is currently called the Right in political struggles is defined less by a positive content than by a generic opposition to the most extreme forms of subversion and social revolution that gravitate around Marxism and Communism. The Italian Right includes diverse and even contradictory tendencies. A significant sign of confused ideas and today's narrow horizons is established by the fact that in Italy today liberals and many other proponents of democracy can be considered as men of the Right, a situation that would have appalled representatives of a real traditional Right, because when such a Right existed, liberalism and democracy were notoriously and justly considered as currents of revolutionary subversion, more or less as radicalism, Marxism and Communism appear today in the eyes of the so-called parties of order.[40]

What is called the Right in today's Italy includes various monarchists, and especially those tendencies with a "nationalist" orientation that are committed to maintaining ideological ties with the preceding regime, that is, Fascism. What has so far been lacking in these tendencies

---

40 The British political theorist John Stuart Mill (1806-1873), in his essay 'On Liberty', wrote that any political system requires both 'parties of order', which represent tradition and conservatism, and 'parties of progress', which represent new ideas and liberalism.

is the necessary differentiation that could allow them to appear as representatives of an authentic Right. This belief is the result of thoughts we shall develop that are devoted to distinguishing the ideological contents of Fascism. Making these distinctions should have represented for this movement an essential theoretical and practical task, which instead has been overlooked.

Do we really need to point out the absurdity of identifying any kind of political Right with the economic Right? Marxist polemics notoriously and fraudulently aim at this identification. For Marxists there is no difference between the Right and the capitalist, or the conservative and 'reactionary' bourgeoisie, which is intent on defending its interests and privileges. In our political writings, we have never grown weary of denouncing this insidious confusion and the irresponsibility of those who, by favouring this confusion to some degree, offer arms to the enemy. *Between the true Right and the economic Right there is not only no common identity, but on the contrary, there is a clear antithesis.* This is one of the points that will be emphasised in the present pages, when we refer to the relations between politics and economy that Fascism tried to define and, what is more, derive from every true traditional doctrine of the state.

As for Italy's history, we have already said in reference to it that, unfortunately, there is very little that can be gathered for defining the true Right's point of view. In fact, as everybody knows, Italy was unified as a nation above all under the banner of ideologies that derive from the Revolution of the Third Estate[41] and from the 'immortal principles' of 1789.[42] These ideologies do not play simply an instrumental and secondary role in the movements of the *Risorgimento*,[43] but were transplanted and prospered in the united Italy of the nineteenth and early twentieth centuries. This Italy has been very far from presenting the political structure of a new, strong and well-articulated state that entered as a latecomer among the great European monarchies.

---

41 In pre-Revolutionary France, the general assembly of the French government was divided into three States-General: the clergy (First), the nobles (Second), and the commoners (Third).

42 The French Revolution, one of the slogans of which was 'liberty, equality, brotherhood'.

43 The *Risorgimento* ('resurgence') is a name for the conquest and unification of the various states on the Italian peninsula by the House of Savoy, the rulers of Piedmont in northern Italy. It included Garibaldi's overthrow of the Kingdom of the Two Sicilies (1864) and culminated in Savoy's unprovoked invasion of the Papal States in 1870.

This 'little Italy' was a land of parliamentary democracy and a domesticated monarchy, where subversive movements, by exploiting social distress and the consequences of an inept administration, succeeded in provoking agitations that were often violent and bloody. There did exist, it is true, the so-called 'historic Right', but it barely held itself upright and lacked the necessary courage to reach the roots of the evils that it should have opposed, even if in the times of Di Rudinì[44] and Crispi[45] it was capable of demonstrating a certain resolute character in the face of those evils. At any rate, it was basically an expression of the bourgeoisie. Unlike the Right of other nations, it did not represent an aristocracy as a political class that represented an old tradition. The tiny vestige of piedmontese[46] aristocracy it had to offer in this sense almost completely evaporated when it passed from the kingdom of Piedmont to the Italian nation. More than in domestic politics and the elaboration of a general doctrine of the state, the historic Right achieved noteworthy success in the field of foreign politics, where its crowning accomplishment was setting up the Triple Alliance.[47] If it had developed in all its logical postulates, this fortunate connection could have removed Italy from the orbit of the ideologies of French and revolutionary origin and oriented her in the direction of those that were, in good measure, preserved in the traditional states of Central Europe. This development could have provoked a re-dimensioning of fundamental political ideas, but it completely misfired. Therefore the historic Right has left us no precise ideological legacy and developed into a moderate liberalism. When the Triple Alliance came to an end and Italy intervened in the

---

44 Antonio Starabba, marchese di Rudinì (1839-1908) served twice as the Prime Minister of Italy during the 1890s. He was blamed by the conservatives for yielding too much to socialist radicals, which led to his dismissal from office. He ordered the violent repression of a strike in Milan in May 1898, which led to the Bava-Beccaris massacre in which many workers were killed and injured.

45 Francesco Crispi (1819-1901) was a Sicilian politician who helped to establish Italian unification. He served twice as Prime Minister between 1887 and 1896. In 1894, he ordered the army to brutally crush an uprising of various liberal factions in Sicily, leading to a suppression of anarchists and socialists throughout the country.

46 Piedmont is a region of northern Italy which initiated Italy's unification following its independence from the Austrian Empire. The House of Savoy, or the governing monarchy of Piedmont, became the monarchs of the Kingdom of Italy.

47 The Triple Alliance, which was formed in 1882, consisted of Italy, Austria-Hungary and Germany, and acted as a counterweight against the Triple Entente of the United Kingdom, France and Russia. It lasted until 1914.

First World War on the side of the Entente Cordiale[48] which defended, in addition to its material interests, the cause of democracy (despite the presence in the Entente of autocratic Russia, which was doomed to pay a tragic price for its guilty politics), Italy returned almost entirely to the direction that she had chosen during the *Risorgimento*, in close connection with the ideologies and international revolutionary movements of 1848-1849.[49] In addition, the nationalist excuse for interventionism was doomed to be revealed as an illusion, if one considers only the political and social climate of 'victorious' Italy, where the anti-nationalist forces had, through their entire term, almost free rein and where no revolution or recovery from above, no constitution of a true Right in legal terms, took place before the arrival of Fascism. In such a climate, what was the possible significance of what Italy gained in terms of the partial territorial payment of irredentist claims?[50]

Our reference to the historic Italian Right that arose in a parliamentary regime leads us to a clarification. Strictly speaking, concerning what we have in view and which will constitute our reference point, the term 'Right' is inappropriate. In fact, it presupposes a duality. Practically speaking, the Right defines itself in the framework of the democratic parliamentary party regime in opposition to a 'Left', and therefore in a framework rather different from the traditional one of the preceding regimes. In such regimes it was possible to have, at most, a system of an English type in its original pre-Victorian form, that is, with a party that represents the government (which is, in a certain sense, the Right) and an opposition, which is understood, however, not as an ideological or principled opposition, nor as an opposition to the system. Rather, it is an opposition *within* the system (or structure) which has the function of rectifying or integrating criticism, without of course questioning the idea of the state, which is in a certain way transcendent and inviolable.

---

48 The Entente Cordiale was a set of treaties signed by the United Kingdom and France in 1904 which laid the groundwork for the Triple Entente, which was created in 1907.

49 A series of revolutions based on liberal and socialist principles broke out in various European countries in 1848. The unrest lasted well into 1849.

50 In April 1915, Italy secretly signed the Pact of London with the Triple Entente, agreeing to switch sides in the First World War in return for a promise that territories in other countries which were regarded as part of Italy, as well as parts of the German and Ottoman empires, would be awarded to it at the end of the war. Italy honored its agreement, but the Pact was nullified by the Treaty of Versailles, and Italy was not granted everything that had been promised in it.

Such a 'functional' opposition, severely limited in an organic and always loyalist context, has nothing to do with an opposition that can motivate one or another of the many parties, with each one depending on itself and aiming at the conquest of power and the state, if not at the founding of an anti-state, as was the case with the Republican Party[51] in the past and as is the case with today's Communist Party.

This is the way it is necessary to conceive the Right taken in its best sense, that is as political and not economic, not as something linked to an already regressive phase, a phase marked by the advent of parliamentary democracy with the regime of many parties. In this phase, the Right presents itself factually as the antithesis of the various Lefts, almost in competition with them on the same level. In principle, however, the Right represents, or ought to represent, a higher demand. It ought to be the recipient and affirmer of values linked directly to the idea of the true state: values that are in a certain sense *central* and superior to every practical opposition, according to the superiority inherent in the very concept of authority or sovereignty taken in its fullest sense.

These hints are already leading to the definition of our reference point, through which it will be permitted to speak, in general, of the great European political tradition, not thinking of a particular regime as a model, but rather of some basic ideas that, in different but coherent ways, have been at the foundation of different states and have never been fundamentally questioned. By an amnesia that is too unusual to be considered natural and should be explained (in the best case scenario, that is, apart from the falsifications and misleading suggestions of a certain type of historiography) as the pathological effect of deep traumatic events, our contemporaries seem to have no longer a living and adequate idea of the world to which has been customarily applied the faded tag of 'old regime'. In this regard, we are evidently not looking at directive principles but at certain incarnations of those principles that are always subject to attrition, denaturing and wearing out, and which in any case have a certain more or less unrepeatable conditionality. But the contingence, and the lesser or greater longevity of similar forms, which naturally are, at a given moment, situated in the past, does not weigh

---

51   The Italian Republican Party was a liberal party which opposed the ascension of the House of Savoy over Italy in the 1860s. Once they established themselves as the monarchs of the nation, the Party responded by refusing to participate in the political process, although it continued to have an important role in affairs. The Party was banned by the Fascists in 1926.

and ought not to weigh against the validity of the principles. This is the touchstone for every examination that aims at collecting the essential and avoids becoming the subject of an *historicist* confusion.

We can therefore bring these preliminary considerations to a close by saying that, ideally, the concept of a true Right, what we mean by the Right, ought to be defined in terms of forces and traditions that acted formatively on a group of nations, and sometimes also on supernational unifications, before the French Revolution, before the advent of the Third Estate and the world of the masses, and before bourgeois and industrial culture, with all its consequences and its games, which consist of actions and concordant reactions that have led to the contemporary chaos and to all that threatens to destroy the little that still remains of European culture and European prestige.

Please do not ask us to be more precise, because that would be equivalent to asking for a systematic exposition of a general doctrine of the state. In part, the reader can refer to our book called *Men Among the Ruins*. Greater precision, however, will become clear as we examine the various topics we shall discuss as we proceed.

II

'Neo-Fascism' is the name given today by both democrats and Communists to the 'national' forces in Italy that are most decisively opposed to both currents. To the extent that these forces accept this designation unreservedly, a situation is created that is full of errors and lends itself, dangerously, to the enemies' game. Incidentally, we owe the acceptance of this name to the talk, obviously in a pejorative sense, of 'nostalgics' and 'nostalgia'. Fascism has undergone a process of what can be called *mythologising*. In regard to it, the attitude taken by most people has an emotional and irrational character, instead of a critical and intellectual one. This is especially true for those who maintain an ideological loyalty to yesterday's Italy. They have made Mussolini and Fascism into objects of a 'myth' and they keep their eye on a reality that is historically conditioned and on the man who was its centre, instead of on political ideas that should be taken seriously in themselves and for themselves, independently of these historical accidents, so as to be able to maintain forever their normative value in regard to a clearly defined political system.

In the case we are now discussing, mythologising has naturally had as its counterpart *idealising*, that is, emphasising only the positive sides of the Fascist regime, while intentionally or unconsciously ignoring the negative sides. The same procedure is practiced in the opposite direction by the anti-national forces for a mythologising having instead as its counterpart systematic denigration, the construction of a myth of Fascism in which only the most problematic sides are tendentiously emphasised so as to discredit all of it or to make people hate it.

In the second case, it is well-known that bad faith and partisan passion are manifestly at the basis of a further procedure and a style of arguing deprived of all legitimacy. They claim, that is, to establish a causal nexus between what exclusively concerns the ups and downs and consequences of a lost war and the intrinsic value of Fascist doctrine. For any rigorous thinking, this kind of nexus is absolutely arbitrary. We have to assert that the eventual value of Fascism as doctrine (apart from a given international politics) is as little prejudiced by the results of a lost war as it would be proven or confirmed by a war that, instead, was won. The two planes of principle and historical contingency are absolutely distinct, with all respect to the historicist dogma *Weltgeschichte ist Weltgericht*,[52] the favourite slogan of men who lack a backbone.

Beyond any partisan one-sidedness, those who, unlike the 'nostalgics' of the new generation, were alive during the Fascist period, and so have a direct experience of the system and its men, know and acknowledge that not everything was in order in Fascism. As long as Fascism existed and could be considered as a restorative movement in progress, with its possibilities not yet exhausted and crystallised, it was only fair not to carry criticism beyond a certain point. Those who, like us, while defending an order of ideas that coincided only in part with Fascism (or German National Socialism), did not condemn these movements (despite being well aware of their problematic or deviant aspects), did so counting precisely on further possible developments — to be enthusiastically favoured by every means — that would have rectified or eliminated these problems.

Today, when Fascism stands behind us as a reality of past history, our attitude cannot be the same. Instead of the idealisation appropriate to 'myth', we need to separate the positive from the negative, not only for theoretical ends, but also for a practical orientation for a possible political struggle. Therefore it is not right to accept the epithet of 'Fascist' or 'neo-Fascist' *tout court*.[53] We should call ourselves Fascist (if we decide to do so) in relation to what was positive in Fascism, but not Fascist in relation to what was not positive in Fascism.

Readers need to bear in mind that, apart from the positive and negative elements in the character of Fascism which we have just mentioned, a movement susceptible to development contained several different tendencies, and only the future could have told us which ones would have prevailed, if military defeat and the internal collapse of the nation had not paralysed everything. In Italy — and Germany, too — national unity did not exclude significant tensions within the system. We are not alluding here to simple ideological tendencies represented by one group or

---

52 German: 'World history is the world's tribunal', an expression that was coined by Schiller and later used by Hegel.

53 French: 'in short', here used in the sense of 'without qualification'.

another. Such tendencies were, for the most part, of little significance, and we shall ignore them in the present examination. We are dealing rather with elements that concern the structure of the Fascist system and regime, taken concretely, in its governmental and, generally, institutional reality. This is the second and more important reason for the need to overcome mythologising and not to take Fascism in an undifferentiated manner. If, then, one thinks of the two fascisms, the classic form of the 'Twenty Years' from 1922-1943[54] and the Fascism of the Italian Social Republic (1943-1945),[55] which were, indeed, united by a continuity of loyalty and willingness to fight, but are, on the other hand, notably different as political doctrines, partly because of the fatal influence of circumstances, it will be even clearer how much the problems of discrimination and 'myth' lead to dangerous conclusions that prejudice a decisive and coherent alignment.

Concerning this issue, the point that must be emphasised is the need to broaden horizons and have a sense of distance. The reality of today is that, while one group considers Fascism as a simple 'parenthesis' and aberration in our more recent history, others resemble people who have been born today and believe that nothing has existed before yesterday. Both these attitudes are inadequate, and we must energetically oppose anyone who claims that the choice must be between Fascism or anti-Fascism in an attempt to exhaust every political possibility and discussion. One consequence of this simple polarity is, for example, that no one can be anti-democratic without automatically being 'Fascist' — or Communist. This closed circle is absurd, and in this connection we must return to our initial considerations, by denouncing the myopic perspective it implies.

Even in looking for positive elements in Fascism, there is an essential difference between two different positions. On the one hand, there are those who take Fascism for their one and only reference point, and make

---

54 *Il Ventennio* ('The Twenty Years') is a common expression for the period between the 'March on Rome' in October 1922, when Mussolini was appointed as the leader of Italy by the King, and July 1943, when he submitted his resignation to the King.

55 The Italian Social Republic, also sometimes known as the Salò Republic due to its being headquartered there, was the government of Fascist exiles which was set up in northern Italy, with German military support, following the occupation of the south by the Allies. Once Mussolini was instated as its head of state in September 1943, Mussolini returned to his socialist roots, and said that he had been prevented from realising the genuine Fascist revolution by political contingencies, and pledged to create a new Fascist state that was much more republican and socialist in nature.

their own political, historical and doctrinal horizon begin and end with
Fascism (as well as analogous movements in other countries — German
National Socialism, Belgian Rexism,[56] the early Spanish Falange,[57]
Salazar's regime in Portugal,[58] and the Rumanian Iron Guard;[59] it was
only the other day that one could speak of a 'worldwide revolution' as
of a general movement in opposition to the proletarian revolution). On
the other hand, there are those who consider what was present in these
movements in terms of particular forms that were more or less imperfect
and adapted to circumstances, but in which ideas and principles of that
earlier tradition of which we have spoken were manifested and active. (In
these ideas and principles we should recognise a character of 'normality'
and consistency.) These people lead these movements' original aspects,
which are 'revolutionary' in the strict sense, back into the domain of
the secondary and contingent. In brief, it is a question of reconnecting
Fascism wherever possible with the great European political tradition,
and to separate out that which existed in it only because of compromise,
of divergent and absolutely deviant possibilities, and of phenomena that
in part suffered from the same evils it was reacting against and attempt-
ing to combat.

[NOTE: A vast literature on Fascism exists, with a corresponding variety of interpretations, but there cannot be found in it a single work that
follows this point of view. When it is not partisan, it has a sociological,
'historicist' or socio-economic character. The categories it employs are

---

56 The Rexist movement was a fascist movement with a strongly Catholic character
    founded by Léon Degrelle in 1930. Following the occupation of Belgium by the
    Germans in 1940, the Rexists divided into two camps, one of which resisted the
    occupiers, the other, including Degrelle himself, having collaborated with them.

57 The Falange was founded by José Antonio Primo de Rivera in 1933. In 1937,
    following the execution of Primo de Rivera during the Spanish Civil War, the
    leadership of the Falange passed to Francisco Franco, who unified the movement
    with other nationalist groups, stripping it of much of its fascist character.

58 António de Oliveira Salazar became Prime Minister of Portugal in 1932. He
    redesigned the Portuguese constitution along corporatist lines, calling his form of
    government the 'New State'. The New State persisted until 1974, when it was
    dissolved following a military coup.

59 The Iron Guard, or the Legion of the Archangel Michael, was a militant revolu-
    tionary group formed by Corneliu Codreanu in 1927. It was strongly anti-
    democratic, anti-capitalist, anti-Communist, and anti-Semitic. It differed from other
    European Right-wing movements of the period due to its spiritual basis, as the Iron
    Guard was deeply imbued with Rumanian Orthodox mysticism. They succeeded in
    taking power in Rumania for four months in 1940, but were soon ousted in a coup.

those of a 'modern' mentality that, as such, ignores the principles that are the basis of our discrimination and the very significance of a true Right. Probably the most complete and recent review is contained in Renzo De Felice's book, *Le interpretazioni del fascismo* (Laterza: Bari, 1969).[60] We do not understand how the author can say (p. 6)[61] that the present work, which he cites (in its first edition), has opposed nothing to current interpretations, which he calls 'classic' interpretations, of Fascism. The point of view we follow, which is not a simple interpretation, but is essentially discriminating and normative, constitutes a fundamental difference. Anyhow, De Felice has stated that he 'does not linger over all aspects of Fascist reality, nor, even less, the directly ideological one', while it is precisely this 'ideological' aspect (which we prefer to call doctrinal) that we hold to be essential, and take most especially into account.]

Today, when we do not have the concrete reality of Fascism in front of us in its specific and challenging historical situation, all this is certainly possible, and also indicates the only way that is practically offered to 'national' forces, given that 'nostalgia' and mythologising are of little use, and since it is impossible to bring Mussolini back to life or have a new one custom-made. The present situation is different from the circumstances that made Fascism possible in its historical aspect.

In the terms I have indicated, it is not difficult to discover the possible superior significance assumed by that discrimination—which is obviously also an integration—of Fascism (and its integration into the traditional legacy). Beyond every confusion and weakness, it offers a touchstone for possible vocations. A great mind of the nineteenth century, Donoso Cortès,[62] spoke of the times that lay ahead for Europe, and which were heralded by the first revolutionary and socialist uprisings, as times 'of absolute negations and sovereign affirmations'. Despite the

---

60   Renzo De Felice, *Interpretations of Fascism* (Cambridge, MA: Harvard University Press, 1977).

61   The passage reads, 'It is, however, a fact that during [the 1960s] – despite these discussions, which were especially lively in Italy and in Germany – the debate in Europe on Fascism continued to revolve substantially around these [older] interpretations; other voices were virtually silent. Even the Fascist survivors have been unable to confront these interpretations with one of their own.' In a footnote appended at the end of it, De Felice cites the first edition of the present book as an example of this, without further explanation.

62   Juan Donoso Cortès (1809-1853) was a Spanish Catholic political thinker who opposed the ideals of the French Revolution.

depths in which we find ourselves, it is still possible to have this sentiment today.

As for the matter of the brief examination that we are about to undertake, it will be limited to what became structural and institutional reality, the regime and the concrete praxis that led from the various forces
that nourished the Fascist movement with regard to the principles that
can be gathered from all this, directly or indirectly. Since the centre of
crystallisation of these forces was Mussolini, we shall refer to the positions of Mussolini for an understanding of Fascist doctrine, which are
defined by means of the internal logic of the movement of which he was
the head, because, as is well-known, unlike Communism and, in part,
National Socialism, Fascism did not have an exactly formulated and
univocal doctrine that preceded action and the 'revolution'. (Mussolini
himself recognised, 'In Fascism, the deed has preceded doctrine.')[63] As
we have mentioned, we shall leave on one side those often discordant
ideological tendencies which remained that way, and which, after the
conquest of power, belonged to particular small groups to which, by
and large, a rather extensive liberty of expression was allowed, probably
due to the fact that their influence was, for practical purposes, almost
non-existent.

---

63   Mussolini expressed this idea in the 1932 essay, 'The Doctrine of Fascism'. This was
     an official article which was composed by Giovanni Gentile and approved by
     Mussolini and published in the *Enciclopedia Italiana* 14 , and which was included
     in Mussolini's *Opera Omnia*, volume 34. The full text is available at www.gutenberg.
     org/files/14058/14058-h/14058-h.htm#THE_DOCTRINE_OF_FASCISM.

III

The fundamental significance that Fascism gradually assumed as it defined itself and triumphed is, from our point of view, that of a reaction, stemming from the forces of the returning veterans and nationalists, in response to a crisis that was essentially a crisis of the very idea of the state, of authority and of centralised power in Italy.

In the period that immediately followed the First World War, Italy presented itself as a secular state, in which the influence of Freemasonry was considerable, with a weak and mediocre liberal democratic government and a monarchy without real power; in other words, constitutional and parliamentary, a state that on the whole lacked a 'myth' in the positive sense, that is, a superior animating and formative idea that could have made of it something more than a mere structure of public administration. It became increasingly obvious that a nation in these conditions was in no position to confront the serious problems imposed by the forces set in motion by the war and the post-war period, nor to combat the revolutionary social lures diffused in the masses and the proletariat by Leftist activists.

Thus, the merit of Fascism was, above all, to have revived in Italy the idea of the state and to have created the basis for an active government, by affirming the pure principle of authority and political sovereignty. This was, so to speak, the positive point of the outcome of the movement as it gradually defined itself and freed itself from its original chief components: a revolutionary veterans' movement, a generically nationalist one and also a semi-Sorelian labour unionism.[64]

According to this view, we could speak of a type of 'vector' reversal and displacement of the momentum of Italian interventionism, the movement to enter the First World War. In fact, in an ideological sense,

---

64 Georges Sorel (1847-1922) was a French philosopher who began as a Marxist and later developed Revolutionary Syndicalism. He advocated the use of myth and organised violence in revolutionary movements. He was influential upon both the Communist and Fascist movements. His primary works are *Reflections on Violence* and *The Illusions of Progress*.

interventionism, as we have emphasised, involved moving Italy into the camp of global democracy, which had joined forces to oppose the Central Powers,[65] and in various aspects was related to the spirit of the *Risorgimento*, the political movement that united Italy, and therefore to the ideas of 1848. Existentially, however, interventionism had its own autonomous revolutionary significance, and the war was an occasion for the awakening of forces that were intolerant of bourgeois Italy, forces like the veterans' movement that nourished Fascism. By rejecting a return to 'normalcy' in this climate, these forces changed poles ideologically and oriented themselves towards the Right, towards the ideal of the hierarchical state and the 'military nation'. Socialist and purely insurrectional (not to say republican) tendencies of the period before the March on Rome were rapidly eliminated. We must put this 'existential' aspect of Fascism in the correct light to evaluate it. As for the other aspect, this was the reason why Mussolini, once he had obtained power, could predict the rise of new hierarchies and speak of a new 'century of authority, a century of the Right, a century of Fascism'.[66] When he affirmed (in 1926), 'We stand for a new principle in [today's] world, we stand for sheer, categorical, definitive antithesis to the world of democracy, plutocracy, Freemasonry, to the world which still abides by the fundamental principles laid down in 1789',[67] he highlighted the 'counterrevolutionary' momentum as one of the most essential aspects assumed by his movement.

Structurally, to a certain degree, one could therefore apply to Fascism the same designation of a potential 'conservative revolution'[68] that was

---

65   The Central Powers consisted of Imperial Germany, the Austro-Hungarian Empire, and the Ottoman Empire (and, later, Bulgaria).

66   In 'The Doctrine of Fascism', Mussolini wrote, 'Admitting that the Nineteenth Century was the century of Socialism, Liberalism and Democracy, it is not said that the Twentieth Century must also be the century of Socialism, of Liberalism, of Democracy. Political doctrines pass on, but peoples remain. One may now think that this will be the century of authority, the century of the "right wing" the century of Fascism.'

67   Mussolini said this in a speech on 7 April 1926, quoted in the Appendix to 'The Doctrine of Fascism', available at www.worldfuturefund.org/wffmaster/reading/germany/mussolini.htm.

68   The Conservative Revolution is a term first coined by Hugo von Hoffmansthal, which has come to designate a loose confederation of anti-liberal German thinkers who wrote during the Weimar Republic. There was a great diversity of views within the ranks of the Conservative Revolutionaries, but in general they opposed both democratic capitalism and Communism in favor of a synthesis of the German (and especially Prussian) aristocratic traditions with socialism. Spengler advocated one form of this doctrine which he termed 'Prussian socialism'. The Conservative

used for trends that arose in Germany after the First World War and before the rise of Hitlerism, and which likewise shared a significant component of veterans. Conservatism here, however, needs to be limited to certain political principles (principles to which the ideology of the French Revolution represented the negation), not to a pre-existing factual reality, because we have seen that in the earlier, pre-Fascist Italy, there was nothing that could give a superior and positive content to conservatism. There was very little that was worthy of being 'conserved'. Unlike the parallel German movement we have just mentioned, in various regards Fascism practically had to start from zero in Italy. This fact also explains, if it does not justify, some of its problematic aspects.

From the point of view of principle, every socialist and democratic ideology was surpassed in Fascist political doctrine. The state was recognised as possessing pre-eminence in respect to people and nation, that is, the dignity of a single superior power through which the nation acquires a real self-awareness, possesses a form and a will, and participates in a supernatural order. Mussolini could affirm (1924): 'Without the State there is no nation. There are merely human aggregations subject to all the disintegrations which history may inflict upon them',[69] and 'The nation does not beget the State [...] On the contrary, the nation is created by the State, which gives the people [...] the will, and thereby an effective existence.'[70] The formula 'The people is the body of the state and the state is the spirit of the people' (1934), if adequately interpreted, brings us back to the Classical idea of a dynamic and creative relationship between 'form' and 'matter' (body). The state is the 'form' conceived as an organising and animating force, according to the interpretation given to 'matter' and 'form' in traditional philosophy, starting with Aristotle.

Therefore, this view rejects the hollow conception of a state which is supposed to limit itself to protecting the 'negative liberties' of the citizens as simple empirical individuals, 'guaranteeing a certain well-being and a relatively peaceful communal life together', in essence reflecting or passively following the forces of social and economic reality which

---

Revolutionaries opposed liberalism in all its forms, rejected a return to the Kaiser's Reich, and saw Germany as being culturally tilted more towards Russia than towards France or Britain. The standard scholarly study of the Conservative Revolution is Armin Mohler's *Die Konservative Revolution in Deutschland, 1918-1933* (Stuttgart: F. Vorwerk, 1950), followed by many later revisions and re-printings.

69   Speech delivered on 8 August 1924, quoted in the Appendix to 'The Doctrine of Fascism'.

70   Mussolini, 'The Doctrine of Fascism'.

are conceived as its basis. It is also the opposite of the idea of a pure bureaucracy of 'public administration', according to the bloated image of what can be the form and spirit of any individualistic society with purely utilitarian ends.

When Fascism affirmed the trinomial of 'authority, order and justice' next to this basic conception, it is undeniable that Fascism renewed the tradition that formed every greater European state. We know then that Fascism recalled, or tried to recall, the Roman idea as the supreme and specific integration of the 'myth' of the new political organism, 'strong and organic'. The Roman tradition, for Mussolini, was not supposed to be rhetoric and tinsel, but an 'idea of force' and also an ideal for the formation of the new type of man who ought to have power in his hands. 'Rome is our starting point and our point of reference; it is our symbol or, if you prefer, our myth' (1922).[71] This statement bore witness to a precise choice of purpose, but also a great audacity. It was like building a bridge over a hiatus of centuries, to regain contact with the only truly valid legacy of all the history that has taken place on Italian soil. A certain positive continuity, however, was established only to a limited degree concerning the significance of the state and authority (*imperium*, in the Classical sense) and also in relation to a virile ethics and a style of rigour and discipline that Fascism proposed to Italians. In official Fascism, however, there was no place for a deepening of the further dimensions of the Roman symbol—symbolic dimensions in the true sense, of a worldview—and the clarification of the Roman character to which it should properly be referred. The elements that could have undertaken this task were either non-existent or were not utilised.

[NOTE: For this clarification it would have been necessary to also confront the problem of the relations between that which was classically Roman and Christianity (and Catholicism), something Mussolini always avoided out of political prudence. (One of our writings from that time,[72] which posed the problem in an extreme way, found no echo in the right place.) About the other point, referring to the further dimensions of the Roman symbol, it is significant that the best the regime could do was to

---

71 From a speech given by Mussolini on 21 April 1922, quoted in Peter Godman, *Hitler and the Vatican* (New York: Simon & Schuster, 2004), p. 10.

72 Julius Evola, *Heathen Imperialism*.

support the so-called Institute of Roman Studies,[73] whose activities were kept to the agnostic ones of philological, archaeological and mediocre learned exercises, without any direction of political, ethical or spiritual effectiveness, so much so that this Institute exists to this day, in anti-Fascist democratic Italy, in the identical form of yesterday.]

---

73 The Institute was created by the Fascists in 1925, intended to help connect Fascism's pedigree to that of the Roman Empire. It continues to exist today, albeit with very different goals.

IV

In the essential lines of its doctrine of the state, which we have just discussed, Fascism's message should be considered, from the point of view of the Right, absolutely positive. We find ourselves right in the orbit of healthy, traditional political thought, and it is starting from this point that the partisan polemic against Fascism, which is one-sidedly denigrating, should be clearly rejected. There is another side to the story, however. On the one hand, it is a good idea to clarify what ought to have been the ultimate implications of the doctrine, which should have been accentuated to assure it a clear character. On the other, it is necessary to indicate the points in which the principal deviations are manifested in the Fascist system and its praxis.

Concerning the first point, we shall limit ourselves to emphasising that the principle of the pre-eminence of the state before everything that is simply people and nation should be articulated further through the ideal opposition between state and 'society'. Under the term 'society' are united all those values, interests and dispositions that enter into the physical and vegetative side of the community and the individuals that compose it. In reality, there is a fundamental antithesis of doctrine between political systems that focus on the idea of the state and those that focus on the idea of 'society' (the 'social' type of state). The second type of system includes the varieties of theories based upon the concept of natural rights, contract theory with a utilitarian base, and democracy, with the related developments that stretch from liberal democracy to the so-called 'people's democracies', that is, Marxist and Communist ones.

Connected to this dualism is the definition of the political level as such in terms, so to speak, of 'transcendence'. Here, the question arises of the 'heroic' or military content, of service as honour and loyalty in the higher sense that can achieve existence with reference to the state, or at least some aspects of existence. We are dealing with a certain ideal high tension that brings us not only beyond hedonistic values (those of simple material well-being), but also eudemonistic ones (that is, ones including spiritual well-being). It is undeniable that Fascism strove to emphasise this dimension of political reality (which we should distinguish from the purely 'social' dimension), as well as the aspiration for an existence that was anti-bourgeois, combative and even dangerous (the famous 'live dangerously',[74] taken by Mussolini from Nietzsche: all this was an echo of the existential component the veterans of the World War brought to the Fascist movement). There was also the demand to integrate man through means of an 'immanent relation to a higher law, endowed with an objective will transcending the individual and raising him to conscious membership of a spiritual society'.[75] The formulation of this demand is significant, even if its content was never adequately defined.

There are various possible judgments one can make regarding the concrete forms with which Fascism tried to meet this demand so as to consider itself the perfect representative of the doctrine of the state we have just discussed. Recognising the superficial and contrived character of the various initiatives and customs of Fascist Italy should not provide a pretext for neglecting a problem which is of fundamental importance no less now than then. It is basically a question of the problem of how to confront an impulse of 'self-transcendence' that can be repressed and silenced, but never completely eliminated, except in the extreme case of systematically degrading people into a bovine state. Yesterday's 'nationalist revolutions' tried to furnish a political centre to crystallise this impulse (again, this is the action we have mentioned of 'form' on 'matter'), to impede its running wild and its onset or breaking out into destructive forms. Indeed, no one can ignore the deep crisis of the 'rationalising' of existence attempted by bourgeois culture, given the many examples of the emerging of the irrational or 'elemental' (in the sense of the elemental character of a force of nature) through the fissures of this culture on every level.

Today, with the return of this obsession with 'rationalising', there is a tendency to render service to an ideal that is not political but 'social' and which belongs to physical comfort, and to marginalise and discredit everything that is comprised of existential tension, heroism and the galvanising force of a myth. But it has been correctly pointed out that

---

74   'For – believe me – the secret for harvesting from existence the greatest fruitfulness and the greatest enjoyment is – to *live dangerously!* Build your cities on the slopes of Vesuvius!' From Friedrich Nietzsche, *The Gay Science* (Cambridge: Cambridge University Press, 2001), section 283, p. 161.

75   Mussolini, 'The Doctrine of Fascism'.

a profound crisis is inevitable at the point when prosperity and comfort will finally become *boring*. The early signs of this crisis are already apparent. They consist of all those forms of blind, anarchic and destructive revolts embraced by a youth that, precisely in the most prosperous nations, notice the absurdity and senselessness of an existence that is socialised, rationalised, materialistic, and dominated by the so-called 'consumer culture'. In these revolts, this elementary impulse finds no object and, left to itself, becomes barbaric.

In traditional societies, there has always existed a certain liturgy or mystique of power and sovereignty that was an integral part of the system, and which furnished a solution to the problem we have been addressing. So there is no good reason for heavy-handed accusations against the initiatives taken by Fascism and its desire to maintain a general climate of high tension. We should rather recognise the line beyond which there is only self-parody or insincerity in a system limited by the incongruity between principles and intents, on the one hand, and a given human substance, on the other.

Strictly speaking, in this context we confront a problem that we can only touch on in the present investigation. We are referring to the accusation that a political system of the type with which we are now dealing usurps a religious significance, that it diverts the human capacity for belief and self-sacrifice and, in general, its power for self-transcendence from its legitimate object, which would be precisely religion, and directs it towards secular surrogates. Clearly, insofar as this objection has weight, it begins from a substantial and insuperable dualism between the world of the state and the spiritual world, the world of the sacred. So it is necessary to see clearly what such a dualism entails. It implies, on the one hand, desecrating and reducing to the material all that is politics, power and authority and, on the other, denying reality to all that is spiritual and sacred. This is also the natural consequence of the command, 'Give unto Caesar'.[76] All the attempts of political theology to cover over the rift it has created lead only to compromise. On the other hand, we need to recognise that this schism was not known in a whole series of traditional political organisms in Europe and elsewhere. In traditional states, one or another form of the consecration of power and authority constituted the fulcrum and legitimation of the entire system. If author-

---

76 Matthew 22:21: 'Render therefore unto Caesar the things which are Caesar's; and unto God the things that are God's.'

ity and sovereignty do not possess some type of spiritual chrism[77] in principle, they do not even deserve to be called by these names, and the entire system of the true state turns out to lack any solid gravitational centre for everything that cannot be reduced to a mere administrative and 'social' system instead of contributing to the climate of high tension we have discussed.

The general situation of the epoch, and the significance that Catholicism as a social force had in Italy, were bound to prevent Fascism from directly confronting the serious problem of the ultimate chrism of the state, although it ought to have been led to confront it, *inter alia*, also by the natural implications of a true, courageous revival of the Roman idea. So, in fact, it continued to oscillate back and forth. On the one hand, Mussolini repeatedly claimed for Fascism a 'religious' value, but, on the other, he did not specify what that religious character ought to be, insofar as it was associated with the political idea and therefore was different from a common, shapeless devotion aimed at what is above this world. He announced that 'the state has no theology, but it has a morality'. This statement, too, is ambiguous, because every morality, if it is to have a profound justification and an intrinsically normative character, if it is not to be a mere convenience of communal living, must have a 'transcendent' basis, through which it brings us to a plane no different from the religious one, where 'theology' too receives its form. So, especially where the education and formation of the new generation were relevant, it was only natural that there were often conflicts between Fascism and the representatives of the dominant religion, who were intent on monopolising everything that had a properly spiritual character by relying on the provisions of the Concordat of 1929.[78]

On the other hand, it is sufficiently clear that, unless we confront this problem, it is not possible to reject completely certain interpretations of movements of the 'fascist' type that see them as a regime of surrogates in a desacralised world, in the context of modern secularised and 'pagan' cults. In this way, even elements like struggle and heroism,

---

77 A type of anointing oil used in many branches of Christianity.

78 In 1929, an agreement was signed between the Vatican and the Italian government at the instigation of Mussolini. In addition to regularising relations between the state and the Church, which had been at odds since 1870, it also granted the Vatican political independence from the Kingdom of Italy for the first time in the modern era. It was one of the signal triumphs of Mussolini's first decade in power. Evola wrote *Heathen Imperialism* in opposition to it.

loyalty and sacrifice, contempt for death, and so on can take on an irrational, naturalistic, tragic and dark character (Keyserling[79] talked about
a *telluric* colouring of the 'worldwide revolution'), when this higher and,
in a certain way, transfiguring reference point is lacking, of which it is
said that it necessarily belongs to a level that transcends the domain of
simple ethics.

Passing to another subject, syncretism, we must point out that, if
in Fascist doctrine there was a sufficient emphasis on the opposition
we have mentioned between what is political and what is 'social', an
analogous opposition was not formulated specifically in regard to a
nationalism that appeals to simple sentiments of fatherland and people,
which is associated with a 'traditionalism' that, because of the character
of the preceding history of Italy, could have nothing in common with
Tradition understood in a higher sense,[80] but was associated with a
mediocre conservatism of the bourgeois variety: priggish, superficially
Catholic and conformist. The nationalist current began with reference points like these, and tried to organise as political activists (the
'Blueshirts')[81] against subversive movements in Italy. Their joining
the Fascist movement contributed to a certain blurring of the Fascist
political idea. Of course, we cannot neglect the conditional character
to which politics is subject, since it is the 'art of the possible'. In recent
times, the pathos of the 'fatherland' and the appeal to 'national' sentiments in the struggle against currents of the Left has been one of
the few useful means left. Thus in contemporary Italy, the 'nationalist'
stance often counts as synonymous with a 'Rightist stance'. From the
point of view of principles, however, we have here a confusion analogous to the one we have already observed for which liberalism, long a

---

79 Count Hermann Graf von Keyserling (1880-1946) was a German philosopher from
    Estonia who wrote about his extensive world travels. He rejected organised religion,
    and in 1920, he founded his 'School of Wisdom' at Darmstadt, Germany, which
    taught that wisdom could be gained from a syncretic approach to religion and
    philosophy. He also preached pacifism and democracy, and opposed the National
    Socialists. He was very influential in his day.

80 Evola here used the term Tradition in the same sense as René Guénon; namely, as
    a set of transcendental metaphysical principles which lies at the heart of all
    authentic religions, and which remains the same even when there are differences in
    the exoteric practices and doctrines. Evola fully explicated his doctrine of Tradition
    in his 1934 book, *Revolt Against the Modern World*.

81 The Italian Nationalist Association, founded in 1910, was Italy's first nationalist
    party, and sought to appeal to the working class as well as the wealthy. The
    Blueshirts were its paramilitary arm. It merged into the Fascist Party in 1923.

bête noire[82] for men of the Right, can today be considered as a Rightist position.

Historically, the connection between 'nationalist' movements and revolutionary ones based on the principles of 1789 is undeniable, even without going back to the distant period in which the erosion of Medieval feudal and imperial culture in Europe provoked the rise and emancipation of 'nations', even as monarchical national states. From the point of view of doctrine, it is very important to understand the naturalistic and, in a certain way, pre-political character that the sentiments of fatherland and nation present (a pre-political and naturalistic character similar to that of the sentiment of family), compared especially to what instead unites men on the political level on the basis of an idea and a symbol of sovereignty. At any rate, every patriotic pathos will always have something collectivising about it. It calls to mind what has been called 'the mob condition'. We shall come back to this point. Right now we believe it legitimate to say that there was confusion in regard to the significance that the myth of the nation in general had in Fascism, which was accompanied by the corresponding slogans and extensions bordering on populism (apart from what can be attributed to the integration of the earlier nationalist party, which we just mentioned). If the syncretism of all this with the doctrine, which we clearly formulated and explained in its traditional meaning, of the pre-eminence of the state in respect to the nation can be considered a characteristic of Fascism as a factual reality, this does not change the fact that, according to pure Rightist thought, there is hybridism in this commingling, and that its components must be distinguished and related to two very distinct ideological worlds.

Given most people's mentality, this clarification in regard to the value of the concept of fatherland and nation, for the goal of purifying the ideal of the true state, could not be emphasised. Still, it will perhaps be helpful to observe how easy it would be to abuse the appeal to fatherland and nation using an impudent and bombastic rhetoric for the most disgraceful ends. We see it today in the patriotism on display in Italy for tactical and electoral ends even by political parties that, in their essence, tend not only to oppose the state but also to negate the higher content that can eventually be gathered by a purified and dignified nationalism. After all, in Russia they can talk of the 'Soviet fatherland' and yesterday,

---

82 French: 'black beast'. The expression signifies something that is particularly and strongly disliked.

in the war of the Soviets against Germany, they were able to make an appeal to the patriotism of the 'comrades'. This is a real absurdity, if we look at things from the point of view of pure Communist ideology. Finally we can notice that, despite the syncretisms we have indicated, the idea of the transcendent reality of the state did not fail to be noted as a characteristic of Fascism, which differentiated it from similar movements. For instance, it was often felt as its distinctive, 'Roman', element when compared to the National Socialist ideology in which the emphasis fell rather (at least in doctrine) on the people-race and the so-called *Volksgemeinschaft*.[83]

[NOTE: We remember on this subject a conversation we had in Bucharest in 1938 with Corneliu Codreanu,[84] the leader of the Rumanian Iron Guard, one of the brightest and most idealistic figures of the 'nationalist' movements of the preceding period. To indicate the differences between Fascism, National Socialism and his own movement, Codreanu referred to the three principles of a human organism: its form, its vital force and its spirit. He said by way of analogy that a movement of political resurgence, while not neglecting the other two, could appeal especially to one of them, in the vaster organism corresponding to the nation. For him, Fascism had concentrated its interest on the element of 'form', like the Roman doctrine of the state. National Socialism emphasised the vital force by its references to 'race' and *Volk*.[85] Codreanu himself wanted to start from spirit and give a religious colour, or rather a mystical one, to his movement.]

As for the dangers presented by the Fascist system from the point of view not of a shapeless liberal democracy, but rather of a true Right, perhaps the most serious one is its so-called totalitarianism.

---

83 In German this references the concept of 'the people's community'. During the National Socialist era, this was related to the idea of the people being rooted in the specific 'blood and soil' of the German nation, and of the abolition of class differences.

84 Corneliu Codreanu (1899-1938) was originally a lawyer, who began agitating against democracy and Communism in the new Rumanian state after the First World War. After he became a threat to the existing regime, he was arrested and executed. Evola met with him in Bucharest shortly before his death. Evola's essays recounting their meeting have been published in English as appendices to Corneliu Codreanu, *The Prison Notes* (United States: Reconquista Press, 2011).

85 German: 'people', as in the people of a nation.

The principle of a central authority that cannot be controverted becomes 'sclerotic' and degenerate when it is affirmed through a system that controls everything, regiments everything and intervenes in everything according to the noted formula, 'Everything in the state, nothing outside the state, nothing against the state.'[86] Where it is not made clear *in what terms* it is necessary to conceive this inclusion, a formula like this can be valid only in the context of Stalinism of the Soviet type, given its materialist, collectivist and mechanistic premises; not for a system of the traditional type based on spiritual values, the recognition of the significance of the person and the hierarchical principle. It is only in a political polemic that it is possible to imagine a common denominator between totalitarianism of the Right and totalitarianism of the Left, which is a real absurdity.

The traditional state is organic, but not totalitarian. It is differentiated and articulated, and admits zones of partial autonomy. It coordinates forces and causes them to participate in a superior unity, while recognising their liberty. Exactly because it is strong, it does not need to resort to mechanical centralising, which is required only when it is necessary to rein in a shapeless and atomistic mass of individuals and wills, from which, however, disorder can never be truly eliminated, but only temporarily contained. To use a happy expression of Walter Heinrich,[87] the true state is *omnia potens*, not *omnia faciens*;[88] that is, it keeps at the centre an absolute power that it can and must use without obstacles in cases of necessity and ultimate decisions, ignoring the fetish for the so-called 'rule of law'. It does not, however, meddle with everything, it does not substitute itself for everything, it does not aim at a barracks-style regimentation of society (in the negative sense), nor at a levelling conformism instead of free acknowledgement and loyalty. It does not proceed by means of impertinent and obtuse interventions by the public sphere and the 'state' into the private sphere. The traditional image is

---

86   This phrase, which became a Fascist slogan, was first used by Mussolini in a speech on 26 May 1927, quoted in Benito Mussolini, *Fascism: Doctrine and Institutions* (Rome: Ardita, 1935), pp. 38-40.

87   Walter Heinrich (1902-1984) was a Sudeten German economist and sociologist who was active in efforts to unify the Sudeten Germans during the 1930s. He rejected the idea of unifying the Sudetenland with the Third Reich, however, and because of this he was briefly imprisoned in the Dachau concentration camp following its annexation by Germany. He was also a theorist of the corporate state. After the war, he became a noted macroeconomist in Austria.

88   Latin: 'All powerful' but not 'doing all'.

that of a natural gravitation of parts and partial unities around a centre
that commands without compelling, and acts out of prestige with an
authority that can, of course, resort to force, but abstains from it as much
as possible. The evidence of the effective force of a state is found in the
measure of the margin it can concede to a partial, rational decentralisation. Systematic state interference can be a principle only in the socialism
of the technocratic and materialist state.

[NOTE: As a supplementary observation, it can be said that all decentralisation has to act in a disaggregating fashion when there is a lack of
central political power. This is why regionalism (where the region has its
own constitution), the basis of the current democratic regime in Italy – a
weak, ephemeral and hollow regime – is a simple mistake, a clear sign of
political blindness. In addition we should note that the character of an
organic unity cannot be recognised in the Italian 'region'. It is a purely
administrative structure lacking the ties and formative traditions that
characterised, for instance, the various German *Länder*.[89] The Italian
regions are so many segments of the national mass, first rendered formless by democracy.]

In opposition to socialism, the essential task of the true state is creating
a given general, and in a certain sense immaterial, climate, according to
what was found in all preceding regimes. This is the necessary condition for a system in which liberty is always the fundamental factor that
can take form in a way that is virtually spontaneous, and which can
function in the right way with a minimum of rectifying interventions.
In this regard, there is a significant antithesis on the economic level
between the North American model, where the federal government had
to promulgate a strict anti-trust law to fight the forms of piracy and
cynical economic despotism that arose in the climate of 'liberty' and
free trade and, on the other hand, the model of contemporary West
Germany where, because of a different climate, which should be considered largely a residual legacy of earlier regimes and connected to some
racial dispositions, economic liberty is realised in an essentially positive

---

89 Germany is comprised of sixteen *Länder*, being states which retain a degree of
autonomy although they are subordinate to the central authority of the German
federal state.

and constructive sense, without the state intervening to centralise or rein in the market.[90]

Where fascism presented a 'totalitarian' character, we should think of this as a deviation from its deepest and most valid demands. In fact, Mussolini could speak of the state as 'a system of hierarchies'—hierarchies that 'should have a soul' and culminate in an elite, an ideal that is obviously different from the totalitarian ideal. Since we have spoken of the economy—but we shall return to that subject—Mussolini disavowed the so-called 'pan-corporatist' tendency that really had a totalitarian character. The Fascist Charter of Labour openly recognised the importance of private initiative. In addition, we could refer to the very symbol of the lictors'[91] fasces,[92] from which the Blackshirts took the name of the movement for anti-democratic and anti-Marxist revolution and, according to Mussolini's phrase, was supposed to signify 'unity, will and discipline'. In fact, the fasces are composed of distinct branches united around a central axis that, according to an archaic symbolism that is common to many ancient traditions, expresses the power from on high, the pure principle of *imperium*. Therefore it has unity and, at the same time, multiplicity, united organically and in synergy, in visible correspondence with the ideas we mentioned above.

On the other hand, the present Italian democratic state has shown that it can be, under 'social' pretexts, much more invasive into private life and capable of expanding state power than the regime that preceded it—I mean, Fascism. The world of the true state can be properly criticized in the area of the so-called 'ethical state'. We have acknowledged a positive character in the conception of the state as a higher principle or power that gives form to the nation. We spoke a little earlier of the task of creating a given general climate. One of the chief aspirations of Fascism was also to be the principle of a new way of life. To the agnostic liberal

---

90   Evola's contrast between the United States and post-war West Germany is made clearly in Wilhelm Röpke, *Jenseits von Angebot und Nachfrage* [Beyond Supply and Demand], which was translated into English as *A Humane Economy: The Social Framework of the Free Market* (Chicago: H. Regnery Co., 1960), and absurdly promoted by conventional American free market advocates.

91   In Classical Rome, the lictors were bodyguards and assistants charged with protecting the political leadership. While escorting their charges in public, the lictors would carry fasces as a symbol of state power.

92   In Classical Rome, the fasces consisted of an axe embedded in a bundle of sticks held together by a band (see the cover of this volume), representing the power of the unified state, and was often carried in procession.

democratic state, 'a mattress which people take turns using', Mussolini contrasted a state 'which necessarily transforms the people'—and he added, 'even in their physical aspect'.[93]

In all this the danger and temptation was present of direct, mechanical procedures precisely of the 'totalitarian' type. In fact, the essence of what we are dealing with should be thought of in terms analogous to what in chemistry is called catalytic action and in the Far East has the designation, which is only apparently paradoxical, of 'acting without acting', or acting by means of a spiritual influence, not with extrinsic and invasive measures. Anyone with a sufficient sensibility has to notice the opposition between this idea and the direction that belongs to the ethical state as conceived by a certain philosophy, represented essentially by Giovanni Gentile.[94] In this direction, the climate of a state descends to the level of the climate of a secondary school or a reform school, and its type of leader descends to the level of an officious and presumptuous pedagogue. So even if they refer to a particular domain, these words come from Mussolini himself: 'Do not think that the state, as we conceive it and want it to be, should take the citizen by the hand like a father takes his son's hand into his to lead him.' The relationships that exist between the sovereign and his subjects, and also between leaders and followers on the level of men and warriors, relationships based on free adherence and reciprocal respect, with non-interference in what is only personal and which falls outside of what is demanded objectively by the ends of common action, give a further example of opposite and positive action.

Everything in Fascism that had the character of the state acting as a school teacher exercising pressure, not on the political and objective level, but on the level of one's personal moral life, as one of the aspects of 'totalitarianism', should be classed among the deviations of the system. Among all these deviations a typical example is the so-called Fascist

---

93   Mussolini, Appendix to 'The Doctrine of Fascism'.

94   Giovanni Gentile (1875-1944) was an Italian philosopher and educational reformer who was among the most important theoreticians and intellectual spokesmen of Fascism. He applied the Marxist/Hegelian dialectic to the idea of the state, believing that in Fascism the oppositions that comprised the various elements of the state were reconciled within the overarching unity of the state's authority. He was gunned down by anti-Fascist partisans in the Italian Social Republic on 15 April 1944. See A. James Gregor, *Giovanni Gentile: Philosopher of Fascism* (New Brunswick, NJ: Transaction, 2001).

'Pronatalist Campaign',[95] which was odious even if it did not rest on an absurd principle, like the one that said, 'number is power', a principle contradicted by all history known to us, since 'numbers' have always been subjugated by small, dominating groups. Empires have been created by these groups, and not by a demographic overflow of masses of the dispossessed and pariahs flooding over the lands of the rich with no other right but their poverty and procreative incontinence. Apart from a similar misunderstanding of the meaning of 'number', it is an obvious fact that a demographic campaign in Italy, whose population was already excessive, would have been more absurd than in any other nation. In general, prejudices united to irresponsibility are an obstacle to recognising a point whose importance can never be emphasised energetically enough, that is, that the natural, frightening increase in the general population is one of the most basic factors in the crisis and social instability of modern times. When energetic measures from above appear truly necessary for the common good to limit this pandemic ill, and not exacerbate it (as with the Fascist demographic campaign), they should of course be taken.

Associated with this same aspect of the 'ethical state' in Fascism, that is the pseudo-pedagogical side, there was often a preoccupation for 'little morality' instead of a concern with 'great morality', especially in regard to the sexual life, with relevant public measures to repress and inhibit sex. This preoccupation was largely due to the bourgeois component of Fascism, and in its moralism, Fascism—this must be acknowledged—was not very different from a puritanical regime of the Christian Democratic[96] type. But ethos in the ancient sense is something rather different from morality as conceived by bourgeois morality. A 'warrior' culture—and Fascism's ambition was precisely to be the beginning of that kind of Italian culture—is never a 'moralistic' culture, or better, to use Vilfredo Pareto's[97] term, a culture of

---

95 Between 1925 and 1938, the Fascist regime attempted to increase the Italian birthrate by offering economic incentives, such as tax breaks, to families that had more children, and generally attempted to glorify and honor childbirth. In spite of this, the campaign failed to increase the birthrate.

96 Christian democracy is an ideology that emerged in Western Europe in the nineteenth century, and which resulted in Christian Democratic parties forming in several nations. It seeks to apply Christian ethics to social problems. Many of them are still active throughout Western Europe, South America and Australia today.

97 Vilfredo Pareto (1844-1923) was an Italian sociologist whose theories were highly influential upon Italian Fascism.

'virtueism'.[98] Here, too, the liberty of the person must be respected, and we should aim at an ideal high tension, not any sort of 'moralising'.

These thoughts are already leading away from the field of the present considerations. The important point in general is the idea of action through prestige and an appeal to special forms of sensibility, vocation and the interests of individuals, an idea that ought to be part of a true state and its leaders. If the appeal finds no echo, little of what really matters can be attained in another way. A people and a nation will just float away or be reduced to a malleable mass in the hands of demagogues knowledgeable in the art of acting on the pre-personal and most primitive strata of human beings.

While we are discussing these issues critically, since the question of the concept of liberty has arisen, it will be a good idea to add an additional brief reflection on the sense that liberty can have in a state based not on the social contract, but on human will, as the Fascist state wanted to be.

Plato said something that we have already cited on other occasions, that it is a good idea for the person who does not have a sovereign within to have one outside. This insight leads us to distinguish a positive liberty from the purely negative, that is external, liberty which can be equally enjoyed by someone who, although free in respect to others, is not free in respect to himself, that is, in respect to the naturalistic part of his own being. We should add to this the well-known distinction between being free *from* something and being free *for* something (for a given task or a given function). In one of our recent works[99] we indicated that the principal cause of the existential crisis of contemporary man was precisely the attainment of a 'negative' liberty, with which, in the end, one does not know what to do, given the lack of sense and the absurdity of modern society. In truth, personality and liberty can be conceived only on the basis of the individual's freeing himself, to a certain degree, from the naturalistic, biological and primitively individualist bonds that characterise the pre-state and pre-political forms in a purely social, utilitarian and contractual sense. Then it is possible to conceive that the true state, the state characterised by the 'transcendence' of the political level that we have discussed, furnishes a propitious environment for the develop-

---

98 Pareto discusses virtueism in his principal work, *The Mind and Society* (New York: Harcourt Brace, 1935).

99 Julius Evola, *Ride the Tiger.*

ment of personality and true liberty in the sense of *virtus*,[100] according
to the Classical understanding. With its climate of high tension, it issues
a continual appeal to the individual to carry himself beyond himself,
beyond simple vegetative life. Obviously everything depends on giving
appropriate and just reference points to encourage this impulse, so that
the effect is really 'anagogical', that is, drawing upward. (For this, let us
say in passing, it is absolutely inadequate to offer as a reference point an
abstract 'common good' that reflects, in magnified form, the same 'individual good' conceived in material terms.) Once the mistake of 'totalitarianism' has been eliminated, it is therefore important to reject in the
clearest way the accusation that a political system based on authority is,
in principle, incompatible with the values of the person and suffocates
liberty. The liberty that is experienced as negative is only an insipid liberty, formless, small and basically of little interest, and all the arguments
for a 'new humanism' offered by intellectuals and litterateurs with no
centre are futile against this fundamental truth.

To avoid any misunderstanding, and returning to what we have
mentioned a little earlier about the art of demagogues, it is, however,
necessary to acknowledge explicitly that next to the 'anagogic' possibility
there is the 'catagogic' one (heading downward). There exists, that is, the
possibility within the individual for 'self-transcending', escaping from
himself by subordinating his own bonds and more immediate interests,
in a direction that is not ascending, but rather descending. This is what
happens in 'mass states', in collectivising and demagogic movements
with an excitable and sub-rational foundation, which can also give to
the individual the illusory, momentary sensation of an exalted, intense
life, likewise conditioned by sensation, by a regression, and by a reduction of personality and true liberty. There is no lack of cases in which
it is difficult to distinguish one possibility from the other, since the two
phenomena can even present themselves as mixed. But what we have
said furnishes some clear reference points to provide a way to prevent
tendentious attempts to attribute validity to arguments against the political system we are trying to identify by means of positive and traditional
elements (even when these elements remain in the phase of demands and
aspirations), since these arguments can be valid only against a system of

---

100 Latin: 'virtue'. In the Roman world, *virtus* referred to one's masculine qualities, which
were identified with honour, courage and service to the people and the state. To the
Romans, *virtus* was something that could only be had in the public sphere; using
these same qualities in the pursuit of a personal goal was not respected.

a completely different type. We have already spoken of the absurdity of positing parallels when speaking of Leftist totalitarianism. To use the term totalitarianism correctly, the substantial difference could be briefly expressed by saying that totalitarianism of the Right is 'anagogic', while that of the Left is 'catagogic', and that only because both are equally opposed to the limited and hollow regime of the bourgeois individual could a myopic mindset think that they have anything in common.

V

We can reasonably affirm that a true Right without the monarchy ends up deprived of its natural centre of gravity and crystallisation, because in almost all traditional states the principal reference point for realizing the independent and stable principle of pure political authority has been the crown. [NOTE: On the meaning and function of monarchy, compare our essay with this title[101] in Karl Loewenstein's *La monarchia nello Stato moderno*.[102]] If this were the appropriate place, we could demonstrate this point with a series of historical considerations. This insight is particularly valid for the recent past, because those regimes that, although presenting to some degree a regular traditional character, did not have a monarchical structure or a parallel type of leadership, owed their traditional character to situations that belonged to the distant past. For instance, aristocratic and oligarchic republics that existed in other times would be inconceivable in the climate of societies from more recent times, where they would end up being immediately denatured.

Returning, then, to what we said at the beginning about the situation in which a Right generally takes form, we can say that its principal function ought to correspond to a certain degree to that of the system that was previously characterised by a particular loyalty to the crown, since the custodianship of the idea of the state and of authority resided with the crown, even in the context of a constitutional monarchy with a representative system of the modern type ('authoritarian constitutionalism').

So it is appropriate for our purposes to undertake a rapid examination of the relationships that existed between Fascism and the monarchy.

The Fascism of the Twenty Years from 1922 until 1943 was monarchical. On the significance and dignity of the monarchy there exist explicit

---

101 Julius Evola, 'Significato e funzione della monarchia', available at the *Fondazione Julius Evola* Web site (www.fondazionejuliusevola.it/SaggioEvola_Monarchia1969. htm). No English version currently exists.

102 Karl Loewenstein, *La monarchia nello stato moderno* (Rome: Volpa, 1969).

and unambiguous statements by Mussolini that allow the establishment of a connection between the monarchical principle and the new dignity claimed for the state by Fascism, as well as between Fascism and the principle of stability and continuity by which Mussolini sometimes referred to the state, while at others, more vaguely and mythologically, to the 'stock'. To quote him, Mussolini defined the monarchy in terms of 'a supreme synthesis of national values' and 'a fundamental element of national unity'. Republican tendencies (largely in sympathy with socialist ones) were present in Fascism before the March on Rome in October 1922. If eliminating these tendencies should be considered an essential aspect of the process of purifying, dignifying and 'Romanising' Fascism, we have to conceive the return to republicanism of the second Fascism, the Fascism of the Salò Republic, which preferred to proclaim itself 'social', almost in terms of those regressions due to trauma that are often observed by psychopathology. Mussolini's legitimate resentment, and the human, contingent and dramatic factors that acted in those circumstances, can also be adequately acknowledged, but they cannot show in other terms the nature of the phenomenon, if we hold to the level of pure political and institutional values. Therefore, from our point of view, in this respect there is nothing to be gathered from the Fascism of the Italian Social Republic.

Originally Mussolini did not 'seize' power, but received it from the King, and under the conformist institutional garb of entrusting the government to him there was the equivalent of a sort of completely legal investiture. Because of successive developments, for the Fascism of the Twenty Years it was possible to speak of a 'dyarchy', that is, the coexistence of the monarchy with a dictatorship. The prominence the second term enjoyed has allowed the current enemies of the past regime to speak simply of the 'Fascist dictatorship', virtually cancelling out the other term, that is, the role of the monarchy, almost as if it was without any significance.

Criticisms animated by a different spirit have been directed at the system of the 'dyarchy'. On the one hand, there are those who thought they saw in the respect accorded to the monarchy a mistake or defect in the revolutionary force of Mussolini's movement (neglecting, however, to indicate precisely what was supposed to be the true outcome of this movement). The truth is, rather, that if there had been a true monarchy in Italy, a monarchy as a power committed to intervene energetically in every situation of crisis and collapse in the state, and not as a simple symbol of sovereignty, Fascism would have never arisen; there would have been no 'revolution'. The critical situation in which the nation found itself before the March on Rome would have been overcome exclusively and rapidly through a 'revolution from above' (with a possible suspension of constitutional encumbrances), which is the only admissible revolution in a traditional regime, and through a successive reorganisation of structures that had proven ineffective. Since that was not the situation in Italy, other paths had to be followed. It can be said that the sovereign had Mussolini and Fascism accomplish, within certain limits, the 'revolution from above', perhaps because he thought in this way to preserve the principle of 'neutrality', of 'reigning without governing', that had been formulated for the monarch in the final period of liberal constitutionalism.[103]

In terms of pure doctrine, it cannot be said that the dyarchic situation that resulted was necessarily a compromise and something hybrid. Dyarchy can also have a traditional chrism based on precise precedents. A typical example in this regard is the dictatorship as it was originally conceived in ancient Rome, not as a 'revolutionary' institution but as one contemplated by the legitimate and pre-existing system of order, essentially destined to integrate it in case of necessity so that an emergency situation, or the opportunity offered by a particular concentration and activation of existing forces might last. In addition, various traditional constitutions, and not only in Europe, have known dualities that were analogous to that of *rex*[104] and *dux*,[105] or of *rex* and *heretigo* or *imperator*[106] (especially in the military sense of the second term). The first term incarnates the pure, sacred and intangible principle of sovereignty and authority, the second presents itself as someone who, in tempestuous times, or in view of special tasks or ventures, received extraordinary powers in an exposed situation, powers that are not appropriate for the *rex*, because of the character of his higher function. Unlike the *rex*, being *dictator* required the quality of a specially endowed personality, since he

---

103 King Charles Albert of Piedmont-Sardinia, the predecessor to the monarchs of the Italian Kingdom that were to arise later, negotiated the Albertine Statute in 1848, which became the constitution of unified Italy in later years. In an attempt to stem the tide of revolutionary sentiment building in Italy, the Statute established a parliament and limited the powers of the monarch.

104 Latin: 'king'.

105 Latin: 'duke'.

106 Latin: 'commander', a title in the Roman Republic.

could not draw his own authority from a purely symbolic function, *ex officio*,[107] with an 'Olympian'[108] character, so to speak.

In less distant times, particular figures like Richelieu,[109] Metternich[110] and Bismarck,[111] who stood at the side of their sovereigns, reproduced again, in part, this dual situation. In this light, *mutatis mutandis*,[112] as a matter of principle there would not be much to object to against the 'dyarchy' of the Fascist period. On the other hand, Mussolini's dignity would not have been diminished if his activity had been limited to that of a loyal great Chancellor. In fact, on one side this was largely the function he exercised until the Empire[113] was created, not by him, but by the King of Italy.[114] It was up to the monarchy to be more or less jealous of his specific prerogatives (or more precisely of those that would have been natural for him in the new state) in this factual situation. In the system of 'authoritarian constitutionalism' that existed in the Second Reich of Germany, Wilhelm II[115] did not hesitate to fire Bismarck, the 'Iron Chancellor', creator of the unity and new-found power of Germany. Bismarck undertook initiatives that the King did not approve of, which

---

107 Latin: 'by the right of one's office'.

108 Meaning, ruling with authority derived from the deities.

109 Cardinal Richelieu (1585-1642) was a French Cardinal who served as the chief minister to King Louis XIII. He played an important role in centralising the power of the monarchy, quelling domestic unrest, and in France's part in the Thirty Years' War.

110 Prince Klemens Wenzel von Metternich (1773-1859) was an Austrian statesman who was one of the most important European diplomats of the nineteenth century. He was involved in the negotiation of the Treaty of Paris in 1814, which marked the end of the Napoleonic Wars. At the Congress of Vienna in 1815, he was instrumental in establishing the new map of Europe, and the balance of power between the Great Powers which was to last, more or less intact, until the First World War. Although he was generally a reactionary, he did believe that the Austro-Hungarian Empire needed to protect equal rights for all its ethnic groups, and even proposed the creation of a parliament to this end, but he was unable to enact such reforms. He was forced to resign during the Revolution of 1848.

111 Otto von Bismarck (1815-1898) was the Prussian leader who unified the German states into one nation during the 1860s, leading to his becoming the first Chancellor of the German Empire in 1871.

112 Latin: 'necessary changes having been made'.

113 Although Italy had had colonial holdings for many years prior, the Italian Empire was proclaimed on 9 May 1936 following the conquest of Ethiopia.

114 In 1936, after the defeat of Ethiopia, King Vittorio Emanuele III proclaimed himself to be the Emperor of Ethiopia.

115 Wilhelm II (1859-1941) was the Kaiser of the German Empire from 1888 until he abdicated the throne following the collapse of Germany in 1918, at the end of the First World War. He dismissed Bismarck in 1890, due to his disagreement with the Kaiser's intention of granting more rights to the workers.

still allowed Bismarck to be honoured as a hero and as the greatest statesman of the German nation.

Since we are occupied here essentially with doctrine, it is no part of
our task to express a value judgment on the way the crisis of the 'dyarchy'
happened when things in Italy took a turn for the worse, essentially as a
result of violence because of the unfortunate events of the war.[116] Strictly,
that is, from the purely juridical point of view, there is little to object to
in the conduct of Vittorio Emanuele III.[117] We can even admit the existence of a palace conspiracy headed by Acquarone,[118] Badoglio[119] and
others. Formally, Mussolini presented himself to the King as the head of
Fascism, to whom the chief assembly of his movement, the Fascist Grand
Council,[120] had denied their confidence and who, designated by the
King as the head of the government, was now ready to hand in his resignation. It was too easy, however, for the sovereign to retreat to abstract
constitutional prerogatives, as though nothing had happened in the
meantime, and employ the liberal constitutional caricature of the King's
non-responsibility. Something different should have intervened, that is,
the bond of loyalty, which was unwritten but more real for precisely that
reason. The act was carried out by a sovereign who, after all, had agreed
to modifying his dynasty's coat of arms, as the official emblem of the
Kingdom of Italy, by the addition of the lictors' fasces—a clear and sufficient expression of the integrative convergence that had characterised the

116 Following the successful Allied invasion of Sicily in July 1943, and knowing that an
    invasion of the Italian mainland was imminent, the King summoned Mussolini to his
    palace following the vote against him by the Fascist Grand Council, dismissed him
    as Prime Minister, and then had him arrested, on 25 July 1943.

117 Vittorio Emanuele III (1869-1947) was the King of Italy from 1890 until 1946, and
    during the entirety of the Fascist era.

118 Count Pietro Acquarone was a wealthy financier who had begun serving as a
    minister in 1939. He was instrumental in helping to organise the coup against
    Mussolini, on the instructions of the King.

119 Pietro Badoglio (1871-1956) was a general in Mussolini's army. He was appointed
    Prime Minister by the King following Mussolini's overthrow, and held the position
    until June 1944. During the war against Ethiopia in 1935, Badoglio had ordered
    the use of poison gas, and also had his men fire on Red Cross ambulances. He was
    never put on trial for war crimes, however, since the British regarded him as being
    reliably anti-Communist.

120 The Fascist Grand Council was created by Mussolini for the Party in 1923, and then
    instituted as an organ of government in 1928. The Council retained the power to
    appoint all major Party positions, to elect the King's successor, and to recommend to
    the King that the Prime Minister (Mussolini) be removed from office. This was done
    on 25 July 1943, although Mussolini did not recognise their authority to do so.

Twenty Years—and who in that period had allowed the authority of the state to be raised not by a Right—which did not exist—but by Fascism.

This is not the place to judge the treatment to which Mussolini was subjected, nor regarding the way the King kept faith with the declaration, 'The war goes on',[121] nor on the events that followed. We must, however, acknowledge that, faced with all this, those who held that their bond of loyalty to the sovereign had been dissolved and went on to serve the second Fascism can claim an undeniable legitimacy for their behaviour. Equally, we can understand that an all-too-human resentment should have pushed Mussolini towards what history inauspiciously presents so many examples of, to the greater glory of subversion: legitimately taking sides against a person who stretches or arbitrarily changes the principle of which he is only the representative—in the present case, the monarchy. Hence Mussolini's proclamation of the Republic, and, more to the point, a republic called 'social', which we have already compared to the degenerative regressions that are often found in the aftermath of psychic trauma in the individual.

[NOTE: Mussolini proclaimed the Republic—obviously as a result of the force of the sentiments that had built up in him in the semi-detention in which the new government had held him after July 25[122]—by direct personal initiative, without consulting anyone. We can attest this because we were in Hitler's general headquarters at Rastenburg when Mussolini arrived there,[123] just after he was liberated by Otto Skorzeny.[124] He

---

121 Initially, largely out of fear of the large numbers of German forces still present in northern Italy, Badoglio, on orders from the King, insisted that Italy would continue to fight on the side of the Axis despite the removal of Mussolini from office. Secret negotiations with the Allies began, however, leading to an armistice on September 3. The armistice was made public on September 8, to the surprise of the Italian armed forces.

122 Following his arrest, Mussolini was held captive, in secret, at the Campo Imperatore Hotel, a ski resort in the Apennine Mountains.

123 Evola discusses his activities during this period at greater length in *The Path of Cinnabar* (London: Arktos, 2009).

124 Otto Skorzeny (1908-1975) was a famed *Obersturmbannführer* in the Waffen SS during the Second World War. Having determined the location where Mussolini was being held, he was part of a unit, led by Major Harald Mors, who used gliders to attack the hotel, liberate Mussolini and bring him to Germany on 12 September 1943. He remained active after 1945, helping fugitive Nazis through the ODESSA network, and also working with various neo-Fascist groups around the world, and especially in Argentina, in the hope of reviving Fascism. He also created the Paladin Group in 1970, which offered paramilitary training. He counted South Africa, Franco's Spain, the Greek military junta, Libyan Col. Gaddafi, and various Palestinian nationalist groups among Paladin's clients.

immediately met with some Fascist leaders who were there (we were present), with whom he made no reference to the institutional problem. He sent them away at about 9:00 PM. The next morning, towards 8:00 AM, without having talked with anyone, he prefaced the first order of the day with the proclamation of the Republic. We probably should not exclude the influence of Hitler, whom Mussolini saw upon his arrival and before meeting with us. In fact, Hitler had a significant contempt for monarchy in general that was, in fact, incompatible with the *Führer* principle to which we shall return later. We were in Austria at the time of the *Anschluss*[125] and in the following period. We ought to say that what the Nazi *Gauleiter*[126] for Austria was capable of saying in his speeches against the Habsburgs[127] was of a vulgarity in no way inferior to that of a Jacobin[128] or Communist proletarian.]

As a result, through the chain of successive events that in, a certain way, had the character of Nemesis,[129] the monarchy in Italy was doomed to end[130] without even the glimmer of greatness and of tragedy.

---

125 The *Anschluss* (German: 'union') refers to the annexation of Austria, and its subsequent incorporation into the Third Reich, by Germany in March 1938.

126 A *Gauleiter* was the National Socialist Party leader for a specific region of the Reich. Evola is probably referring to Baldur von Schirach, who was the *Gauleiter* of Vienna from 1940 until 1945.

127 The Habsburg monarchy was one of the most important royal families of Europe, providing the monarchs for many of its empires. The last Habsburg monarch was Charles I of Austria, who abdicated in 1918 following the Austria-Hungarian Empire's defeat in the First World War.

128 The Jacobin Club, a political group in eighteenth-century France, was one of the driving forces of the French Revolution. Since then, 'Jacobin' has often been used as a generic term for Left-wing radicals.

129 Nemesis was the Hellenic god of retribution.

130 In 1946, the Italian public's dissatisfaction with the government grew to the point that an election was called to determine whether or not the Kingdom of Italy and its royal family should be dissolved. King Vittorio Emanuele III abdicated in May, before the election, in favor of his son, Umberto II, hoping that a new monarch would help to alleviate the public's fears. This was unsuccessful, however, as the vote the following month still resulted in the dissolution of the Kingdom in favor of a republic, and the expulsion of the royal family from Italy.

VI

After this parenthesis concerning historical contingency, let us return to the structural examination of the Fascist regime. If, from our point of view, we do not believe that the 'dyarchy' represented an absurdity in principle, it is, however, possible to find fault with a more general dual situation in the whole structure, and, in regard to it, our judgment must be different. In fact, by its very nature, a revolutionary movement of the Right after a first phase ought to aim at re-establishing normality and unity on a new level through adequate processes of integration.

Therefore, in the first place, we should mention the hybrid character of the idea of the so-called 'one-party state',[131] insofar as it assumed the character of a permanent institution in the new state. In this regard, we must separate the positive instance that stood at the foundation of this idea and indicate in what more adequate context the Party should have acted after the conquest of power.

The true state — it is hardly necessary to say this — does not admit the rule of parties (*partitocrazia*) of democratic regimes. Parliamentary reform, which we shall talk about in a little while, undoubtedly represented one of the positive aspects of Fascism. However, the conception of a 'one-party state' is absurd. Because it belongs exclusively to the world of parliamentary democracy, it is only irrationally that the idea of a 'party' can be preserved in a regime opposed to everything that is democratic. Saying 'party', on the other hand, means saying part, and the concept of party implies that of a multiplicity, through which the sole party would be the part that wants to become the whole, in other words, the faction that eliminates all the others without, for all that, changing its nature and elevating itself to a higher level, precisely because it continues to consider itself as a party. Yesterday's Fascist Party of Italy, insofar as it gave itself a permanent institutional character, for that reason represented a kind of state within the state, with its own

---

131 The National Fascist Party became the sole party in Italy by law in 1928.

militia, federal police, Grand Council and all the rest, to the prejudice of a truly organic and monolithic system.

In the phase of the conquest of power, a party can have a fundamental importance as a crystallising centre of a movement, as its organisation and guide. After this initial phase its survival as a party beyond a certain period is absurd. We should not think of this in terms of 'normalisation' in the worst sense, with a corresponding collapse of political and spiritual tension. The 'revolutionary' and innovative demand of Fascism placed the task of adequate action upon the substance of the nation in a way that was continuous, general and, in a certain way, pervasive. But then it is in a different form that the valid forces of a party ought to subsist, not to break up, but remain active: by inserting itself into the normal and essential hierarchies of the state and eventually controlling it, occupying key positions in it and constituting, more than an armed guard of the state, an elite that bears, to an eminent degree, the idea. In this last case, more than a 'party' it will be appropriate to speak of a kind of 'order'. This is the same function that in other times was exercised by the nobility as a political class, up to a relatively recent period of the Central European states.

Fascism was committed to maintaining itself as a 'party', for which there was, as we have said, a kind of duplication of government and political articulations. They were almost like superstructures that sustained and supported a building that lacked stability, in place of an organic synthesis and a symbiosis. The gap between party and state was not functionally overcome, for instance, with declaring—as it was declared—that the 'party' and the Fascist militia itself should be 'in the service of the nation'. This cannot be accepted as a valid element of the Fascist system, even if it is not legitimate to hypothesise the future in relation to the developments that the regime could have had if *force majeure*[132] had not provoked its collapse, and even if we must acknowledge the validity of the objection that the existence of forces which did not follow the new course, or followed it only passively, rendered every hasty evolution dangerous in the normalising, anti-dual sense we mentioned before. And what happened after twenty years of this regime is, in this regard, rather eloquent.

---

132 Latin: 'superior force', used in the case of something that is seen as being outside human control.

However, precisely in reference to this last point, we should mention the fact that the conception of the Fascist 'Party' was affected by its origins, that is, by the intrinsic solidarity of the concept of a party with the democratic idea, through the lack of a rigorously qualitative and selective criterion. Even after the conquest of power the Fascist party was committed to being a mass party. It opened itself up, instead of purifying itself. Instead of making membership in the Party appear a difficult privilege, the regime practically imposed it on everyone. Who is there who, yesterday, did not have the 'card'?[133] And, in addition, who could allow himself not to have it if he wanted to perform certain activities? Hence the fatal consequence of countless superficial adherents, who were conformist or opportunistic, with effects that were immediately manifest at the moment of crisis. A retrospective counterproof was constituted by quite a few of yesterday's 'Fascists', not just private citizens, but writers and intellectuals who afterwards changed their colours, trying to put their past in the shadow, denying it, or declaring that they were, at that time, cynically in bad faith. The conception of 'party' in Communism and National Socialism, that was maintained also in those movements, had instead a rather more exclusive and selective character. In Fascism, on the other hand, the idea of a 'mass party' prevailed, prejudicing the positive function that the Party could eventually have continued to have. From our point of view, the positive outcome in conjunctions of this kind, the positive counterpart of the revolutionary concept of 'sole party' in a normalised and integrated institutional context, should instead be thought of in terms of a type of Order, the backbone of the state, participating, to a certain degree, in the authority and dignity that gathers—indivisible—at the top of the state.

This creation of an Order should have been the goal of a movement of national political renewal in the necessary passage from the phase of its conquest of power to the phase in which the same energy is manifested as a natural moving force, which forms and differentiates the human element. Generally, the 'Party's' remnants were obstacles for a complete and enthusiastic development of the Fascist regime in the sense of a true Right. On the practical level, they caused various destructive interferences, as when, on one hand, anyone who had been in the Party,

---

133 Members of the National Fascist Party were issued an identity card. Evola never joined the Fascist Party (or any other). Evola penned an essay with the ironic title of 'Identity Card' in his short-lived journal *La Torre* in 1930, expressing his hopes and his reservations concerning Fascism.

especially during its activist and insurrectional phase (for instance, having been Fascist toughs, *squadristi*),[134] was considered adequate for tasks and functions that needed special qualifications and competence, or even a nearly 'Fascist' mental attitude. On the other hand, the Party was happy to accept men with a certain reputation if they gave their adhesion to Fascism, without caring too much if their adhesion was only formal, and even if they were really agnostic in attitude, or even downright anti-Fascists (as was the case for quite a few members of the Royal Academy of Italy,[135] which was founded by Fascism).

---

134 *Squadristi* was the Italian name for the Blackshirts, the paramilitary arm of the Fascist Party. The *squadristi* were instrumental to Mussolini's assumption of power in the March on Rome in 1922.

135 The Royal Academy of Italy was established by royal decree in 1926, in imitation of the French Academy. It was dissolved in 1943 with the end of the Fascist Party, although a rump version of it existed in the Italian Social Republic, until its defeat.

VII

We cannot pass by in silence a further negative aspect of the system, one that is related to the unresolved or insufficiently integrated dualities we have just pointed out, because unfortunately it has received a great deal of attention in the mythologising of Fascism. So much so, in fact, that unless we pay careful attention to the elements in the system that can be separated from unique historical contingencies, this aspect can seem to constitute one of its most essential characteristics. We are dealing with the phenomenon of the cult of the leader (*ducismo*) represented by Mussolini when we consider in him the quality, conserved inside the system, of the head of a movement and a party, his aiming at a prestige that bordered almost on the tribunician and Napoleonic, the emphasis on his person *per se*; the inclination which was, if not demagogic, at least somewhat democratic, to 'go to the people', not to despise the applause of the *piazza*. After so many 'oceanic' public meetings in front of the Palazzo Venezia,[136] these same people paid him back with a worthy response in 1945.

[NOTE: In general one cannot ascribe as a positive point for Mussolini some statements in which, in open contradiction to many others, instead of absolutely rejecting any idea of democracy, he was almost competing to claim for Fascism the title of 'true' democracy (just as every party in Italy does today, including the Communist Party, and unfortunately some members of Parliament considered neo-Fascist): 'If there has ever been in history a regime of democracy, that is, a people's state, it is ours' (speech given at Perugia on 6 October 1926). And a few years later: 'If there is a country where true democracy has been realised, that country is Fascist Italy' (speech given in Milan on 1 November 1936).]

---

136 The Palazzo Venezia is a palace in the centre of Rome where Mussolini had an office. He gave speeches from its balcony.

There is an obvious inconsistency between this aspect of Mussolini, on the one hand, and, on the other, his doctrine of the state and statements like the well-known ones in the speech he delivered at Udine in September 1922: 'I do not worship the new divinity, the masses. It is a creation of democracy and socialism.'[137]

This emphasis should not seem contradictory in respect to what we have said above about the particular personal qualities and the prestige that a *dux* per se, in his special function, must possess. But here the question arises which we discussed concerning the subject of the specifically 'anagogic' climate to be created in every state of the traditional type. This kind of climate cannot be obtained with lively activities that, while they can reach a level of fanaticism and collective enthusiasm in certain cases, are still based on the sub-personal aspects of man as mass-man and on the art of stirring people up against any other possible form of individual reaction. We must be mindful that, as intense as the magnetism created in this way can be, all the same it does not cease to have an ephemeral character, profoundly different from what can derive from the formative force from above of a true tradition. The mass that can be formed in this way is comparable to the adhesion of so many metal particles attracted by a magnet. When, however, the current that generates the magnetic force field fails, instantaneously all the metal particles drop off the magnet and are scattered in an ephemeral quantity, demonstrating how contingent the preceding state of formless aggregation was. It is in these terms that we should explain most of what happened in Italy and still more in Germany when events destroyed—to continue to use our simile—the current that generated the magnetic field.

Naturally, we may wonder to what degree different techniques of aggregation can be effective today, since the contemporary world is substantially a world of the mass-man. In fact, there is no real, qualitative difference between the phenomenon we are now discussing, which some people would like to make exclusively the fault of certain forms of dictatorship, and, on the other hand, everything that we find present in the political world of anti-Fascist democracy, with its methods of propaganda and demagogy, its 'heap of experts', and the fabrication of 'public opinion'. But granted the validity of this objection and the consequences that can be drawn from it for politics as a mere 'art of the possible' of a

137 Benito Mussolini, *Mussolini: As Revealed in His Political Speeches, November 1914-August 1923* (New York: E. P. Dutton, 1923), p. 148.

more or less Machiavellian type, it does not touch the realm of principles and structures, which is the only one that interests us. For the distinction we are dealing with here, one point is of fundamental importance. Today no one pays attention to it, but there exists a clear chasm between the natural authority of a real leader and an authority based on an amorphous power, and the capacity or art we have talked about of arousing the emotional and irrational forces of the masses, under the influence of an exceptional individual. To clarify, we shall say that in a traditional system, people obey or become rabble or subjects on the basis of what Nietzsche called the 'pathos of distance',[138] that is, because they feel they are confronting someone who is almost of a different nature. In today's world, where the people have been transformed into a mob and mass, obedience is based at most on a 'pathos of nearness', that is, upon equality. People only put up with the leader who is, essentially, 'one of us', who is 'one of the people', who expresses the 'will of the people', who is a 'good friend'. The cult of the leader in the worse sense, as it was affirmed especially in Hitlerism and Stalinism ('the cult of the personality' goes back all the way to Carlyle's confused concept of 'heroes',[139] more or less de-romanticised), corresponds to this second orientation, which is anti-traditional and incompatible with the ideals and *ethos* of the true Right.

[NOTE: It is significant, from a lowering of standards and in order to 'follow the times', as they say, that 'becoming one of the people', and renouncing the prestige of distance, is found not only in the case of sovereigns and members of the nobility that still survive, but also in the religious sphere, as in the behaviour of recent popes, who have identified themselves as 'one of the people'.][140]

138 'Nobody is courageous enough for special privileges these days, for the rights of the masters, for feelings of self-respect and respect among equals – for a *pathos of distance* [...] Our politics is *sick* from this lack of courage!' From Friedrich Nietzsche, *The Anti-Christ, Ecce Homo, Twilight of the Idols* (Cambridge: Cambridge University Press), p. 40. Nietzsche also discusses the 'pathos of distance' in *Beyond Good and Evil*, section 257, and in *On the Genealogy of Morals*, section 1.2.

139 Thomas Carlyle (1795-1881) was a Scottish writer who was extremely influential in the nineteenth century. His book, *On Heroes, Hero-Worship, and The Heroic in History* (1841), portrays human history as being driven by extraordinary individuals.

140 At the time Evola was writing, the reigning Pope was Paul VI, who as an archbishop gained notoriety for preaching to the workers in Milan, which was a centre of Communism, and earned the title 'archbishop of the workers'. He assumed the Papacy during the Vatican II conference, which was the watershed of liberalisation in the Catholic Church. It is also interesting to note that Pope John Paul II was frequently hailed as being 'a man of the people'.

In a certain way we are led back here to what we have pointed out in talking about the reference points that differentiate a traditional system from those that can be distinguished in a system that has a generally 'authoritarian' character. The essential element is constituted by the nature and foundations of the authority, and consequently also by the general existential situation that corresponds to it.

Therefore we can say that in the Fascist regime, what was present institutionally as a dyarchy, or in the other dualities we have mentioned, had an internal counterpart which expressed itself in the coexistence of two distinct centres for rousing the national movement. One presented a populist character that favoured the cult of the leader, and so, despite everything, was basically democratic (after all, we know how often Mussolini favoured a kind of consensus, even when it was clear that it was prefabricated and compulsory) and this democratic residue was often active in the structures of the Party as well.

[NOTE: This observation is relevant to the Fascist Grand Council, insofar as it introduced the democratic principle of voting to its members. Perhaps on 25 July 1943, some of them had organised a conspiracy, which was confirmed by what was being prepared in the circles around the royal family. It was, however, really absurd first to concede the right of a free vote to the members of the Grand Council, and then accuse them of treason and haul them before a court when the majority used this right. If the Grand Council had had the character of a simple advisory body in principle, on 25 July Mussolini could have ignored its majority vote.]

The importance of the democratic element is explained, however, by the weakness of the other centre, the monarchy, with all that could be relevant to a traditional line. So once more we are compelled to acknowledge what prejudiced the system: the weakness of the liberal state that preceded it. But the animating force generated by a different source, namely Fascism, which was the only one capable of elevating the Italian state, gave rise to an ambiguous element on the other hand, because of the (for many reasons) problematic nature of this source. Once more, however, all of this belongs to the field of historical contingency.

It is undeniable that Mussolini was influenced, aside from some of Nietzsche's views, by the theories of Oswald Spengler[141] in those places where he predicted a new era of 'great individuals' of the 'caesarean' type (simplifying, somewhat illegitimately, the complex figure of Julius Caesar),[142] who was destined to succeed the epoch of the democracies. It seems, however, that Mussolini, who must have felt that he was one of these figures, had not paid much attention to the fact that, in Spengler's system, the new 'caesarism', which was very close to 'ducism', in the inferior sense we have discussed, belongs morphologically and situationally to the dark close of a cultural cycle (to the phase of *Zivilization*,[143] which is opposed to the preceding phase of *Kultur*,[144] that is, of a qualitative, differentiated and organic culture, according to Spengler's terminology). It belonged to the sunset, and specifically to the famous 'Sunset of the West', for which in itself, and apart from the character of inevitability that Spengler thought he could recognise, should not be considered a positive phenomenon. To be positive, it would need to be corrected by means of a superior tradition and a diverse chrism. On the practical level, it is anyhow inconceivable that one epoch after the other would follow in direct continuity and at the same level of 'great individuals'. In Italy, the existing possibilities gave rise to an equilibrium or temporary reconciliation with some positive aspects, up to the point where the monarchical Fascism of the Twenty Years found itself subjected to a hard test of strength.

Once these necessary considerations have been made, it behooves us to separate another component in the complex unity of Fascism that, in principle, was of a different spirit, in contrast to everything that stands

---

141 Oswald Spengler (1880-1936) was a German philosopher who is regarded as one of the principal Conservative Revolutionary figures of the Weimar period in Germany. His most important work was his two volume 1918/23 book *The Decline of the West* in which he theorised that all civilisations go through an inevitable cycle of ages of rise and decline in power, with the West currently entering its declining period.

142 Gaius Julius Caesar (100 BC-44 BC) was originally a Roman military commander who seized control of the Roman Republic after waging a civil war, becoming its dictator and transforming the Republic into the Roman Empire.

143 German: 'civilisation'.

144 German: 'culture'. In *The Path of Cinnabar*, p. 204, Evola described Spengler's concepts of culture and civilisation as follows: 'the first term describes the aspects or phases of a qualitative, organic, differentiated and living civilisation, and the latter, those of a rationalistic, urban, mechanistic, shapeless and dispirited one'.

under the banner of the masses and the screaming leaders of the masses. We are referring to the *military* component of Fascism.

These are the words of Mussolini: 'We are becoming more and more a military nation, because we want it. Since we are not afraid of words, we shall add: militaristic. To finish: a warrior nation, that is, endowed in an always higher degree with the virtues of obedience, sacrifice, and dedication' (1934). Before this he had already said (1925), 'Everyone should consider himself a soldier, a soldier even when he is not wearing the grey-green uniform, a soldier even when he works, at the office, at the factory, in the dockyards or on the farm, a soldier linked to all the rest of the army.' On this topic, the reservation we need to make concerns 'militarism'. In addition, we must distinguish between 'military' and 'paramilitary'. The second term can be applied to certain formations that supported the Party in the preceding period, but which were not carefully chosen. As for a certain militarising of existence and the soldier as a general symbol, from our point of view, the traditional point of view of the Right, there is little to object to, once we emphasise in this regard that we are dealing essentially with a style of behaviour, an ethic, that can also have an autonomous value, independently of obligatory military ends. The 'military' training in its positive, living aspects, not what the soldier learns in the 'barracks', must correct everything that can proceed from states of irrational and emotional aggregation by a 'mob' and the 'people ', which we have spoken of earlier. Fascism tried to instil into the Italian people one of the qualities with which, because of its individualism, it was and is less furnished: discipline and love of discipline. In addition, Fascism saw the 'dangers of the bourgeois spirit', and despised 'the stagnation of a vapid existence'. The 'military' orientation had to appear in a natural connection with the political one according to the antithesis, which we emphasised earlier, with which this element stood in respect to the 'social' one. The military style is that of an active and anti-rhetorical depersonalisation. When it is established, it is the most important factor of stability for a political and social organism, just as the army and the monarchy, in their mutual solidarity, have always constituted the essential pillars of the true state before the revolution of the Third Estate, democracy and liberalism. Primo de Rivera[145] could speak

---

145 José Antonio Primo de Rivera (1903-1936) founded the Spanish nationalist party, the Falange, in 1933. In 1936, he was arrested and executed by the Spanish republican government.

of an 'ascetic and military sense of life'.[146] This is a reference point of indubitable value and a touchstone of possible vocations for its adherents. Its antithesis is the climate of the so-called 'culture of affluence' or 'consumer culture', with its spiritually suffocating activity that creates multiple forms of 'protests'.

An essential aspect of the military ethic is the conception and sense of service as honour. It is superfluous to speak of the value this has in the sphere of political and social life. As is known, Fascism introduced the wearing of uniforms for state functionaries, resuming a tradition already existing in other countries, for instance Prussia and Russia. Essentially it was supposed to serve as a symbol to overcome the bureaucratic spirit and to dignify the bureaucracy. To the grey and squalid type of bureaucrat, who dodges every responsibility, for whom service to the state has more or less the same significance as being an employee in a commercial firm or a private business with his eye only on his paycheque and, even more, on his retirement pension (which, before the recent extension of the social security system, was envisioned almost exclusively for public employees), there came to be opposed the type of functionary for whom service to the state was, before anything else, an honour, presupposing, basically, a special vocation, almost as the counterpart to the honour of serving under the nation's flag. To the regressive direction of the bureaucratising of military life, it was possible to contrast the development of 'militarisation' as a means of de-bureaucratising the bureaucracy, this real cancer of democratic and republican states. The uniform of the public functionary could appear, as we have said, precisely as a symbol or a ritual. Lastly, we wanted to indicate the opposite of what belongs to a mechanistic totalitarian system with an example and a simile and, as well, the opposite of the tiresome pseudo-pedagogy or moralism of the so-called 'ethical state'.

The Blackshirts, the rough, woolen uniforms and all the rest are not really part of this development. They are rather part of what in Fascism often had a burlesque or contrived character, which developed out of the the incoherent dualities we discussed out of a faulty sense of due measure and of limits. This is the cause of the ease with which both positive and negative elements mingled in cases that cannot be examined here, because they are part of the realm of contingency.

---

146 From 'What the Falange Wants', a speech originally delivered in Madrid in 1933, available at www.tumblr.com/tagged/jose-primo-de-rivera.

For the same reason it is not appropriate to consider here Fascism's 'militarism', of which we have seen that Mussolini spoke, because he 'was not afraid of words'[147] (although he was perhaps a little carried away by words). In fact, on many other occasions he preferred to speak of a 'strong nation', which is not necessarily the same as a 'militaristic nation'. Naturally, a strong nation has to build its military's potential for warfare, use it when necessary and win the respect of other nations. The nation can consider the possibility of attack and not just defence, depending on the circumstances. That, however, is not a reason for thinking of everything in its 'militaristic' role. The truth is that in the polemic oriented in a democratic and 'social' direction, it makes sense to confuse 'military' with 'militarist'. The real attack is directed against those general values that are not necessarily connected with war, which we have indicated earlier and that include in the first place discipline, the sense of honour, an active impersonality, responsible relationships, command and obedience, a distaste for gossip and 'discussions', a manly solidarity having at its base true liberty—liberty for doing something, something worthwhile that brings you beyond a bourgeois existence that is 'prosperous' and vegetative, not to mention the proletarian existence of the 'state of labour'.[148]

Italy has been liberated in the first place from that heavy burden that appeared to a good part of the Italian people, because of their unhappy dispositions, to be the task of a high tension and a discipline or ethics of a 'military' type that had been laid before them, admittedly in forms that were at times debatable. It is only natural that, in such a 'liberated' nation, those values of a preceding tradition that now survive almost exclusively in the army, and even there in a rather attenuated form, should be systematically threatened and discredited. So-called 'conscientious objectors', who appear in droves, are now treated with 'humane' understanding and, following the absurd ideology of Nuremberg,[149] we

---

147 Mussolini said this in a speech to the Italian General Staff, while discussing Italy's increasing militarisation, on 28 August 1934, quoted in C. J. Lowe & F. Marzari, *Italian Foreign Policy 1870-1940* (New York: Routledge, 2002), p. 400.

148 The Fascists sometimes referred to their regime as the 'state of labour', implying that it was primarily a workers' state. This became an even greater ideal in the post-Fascist Republic of Italy.

149 At the trials of the surviving members of the leadership of the Third Reich which were held in Nuremberg, Germany following the Second World War, many of those accused of 'war crimes' and 'crimes against humanity' defended their actions by claiming that they had only been following the orders given by their superiors. The London Charter was enacted to counter this defense by saying that a soldier can be held accountable for his actions, and that he has a moral obligation to disobey an order that he knows to be unlawful.

sanction the right — no, rather the duty — of soldiers and public officials to refuse to obey orders, and to break their sworn fidelity whenever their own personal opinion suggests it, since the idea of the state should no longer mean anything to them.

VIII

The crisis that Fascism had to confront in the period of the 'Aventine' secession (1924)[150] was a propitious occasion for overcoming the compromise solution represented by the first coalition government. Fascism found itself compelled to confront fully the institutional problem that concerned the representative system and the principle of government. Here, too, doctrine did not precede practice. It was only after various developments that the parliamentary reform was outlined and established in terms of the new corporative[151] Parliament.

'The Chamber of Deputies is now anachronistic even in its very name', Mussolini said in 1933. 'It is an institution that we found, and is foreign to our mentality.' It 'presupposes a world that we have demolished; it presupposes the plurality of parties and the frequent and willing attack on diligence. From the day we abolished this plurality, the Chamber of Deputies lost the essential motive for which it arose'. Mussolini believed that the parliamentary system, 'the product of a definite movement of ideas, as a representative system, is an institution that is now exhausted in its historical cycle'. Inseparably connected with democracy, the parliamentary system in Italy (but also in other states, especially France) had sunk to a level where the politician had been replaced by the party hack, where everyone could see a system of incompetence, corruption and irresponsibility, and where no stability was assured to the state, giving it the

---

150 The Aventine secession refers to the banning of the Socialist Party in 1925, which occurred after a politician from the Italian Socialist Party, Giacomo Matteotti, was killed by Fascists shortly after accusing them of committing fraud in the national elections. The Socialists then boycotted the Chamber of Deputies in the hope of pressuring the King to dismiss Mussolini. Instead, Mussolini banned the Socialist Party, and then began to work against the other parties, eventually leading to the Fascist Party becoming the only party. The secession was named after a similar incident in the government of ancient Rome.

151 Present-day readers may be tempted to think of the term 'corporative' as something relating to companies or business ventures. Evola, however, uses the term, as did the Fascists themselves, to describe a type of society in which its citizens are organised into groups based on the function they perform for the body of the entire society itself, such as agriculture, the military, or administration.

character of an 'empty state', that is, one lacking a substantial centre removed from contingencies. All this indicated the absurdity of the system to Mussolini's eyes.

Strictly speaking, the problem presented a triple aspect: that of the electoral principle in general, that of the representative principle, and, finally, that of the political principle of hierarchy. The Fascist solution was a partial solution. From our point of view, however, the direction can be considered positive.

About the principle of representation and the concept of a parliament, today we have grown accustomed to associating them exclusively with the system of absolute democracy, based on universal suffrage and the principle of one man, one vote. This basis is absurd and indicates more than anything else the individualism that, combined with the pure criterion of quantity and of number, defines modern democracy. We say individualism in the bad sense, because here we are dealing with the individual as an abstract, atomistic and statistical unity, not as a 'person', because the quality of a person — that is, a being that has a specific dignity, a unique quality and differentiated traits—is obviously negated and offended in a system in which one vote is the equal of any other, in which the vote of a great thinker, a prince of the Church, an eminent jurist or sociologist, the commander of an army, and so on has the same weight, measured by counting votes, as the vote of an illiterate butcher's boy, a halfwit, or the ordinary man in the street who allows himself to be influenced in public meetings, or who votes for whoever pays him. The fact that we can talk about 'progress' in reference to a society where we have reached the level of considering all this as normal is one of the many absurdities that, perhaps, in better times will be the cause of amazement or amusement.

Apart from obvious worst cases, it is patently clear, because of the very nature of the democratic principle of representation, that it is impossible to ensure the pre-eminence of a public interest, especially if such an interest involves any transcendental content, 'political' in the opposite sense from 'social', a term now well-known to the reader. In fact, the individual can only have personal interests, or at most the interests of a category. Moreover, given the growing materialism of modern society, these interests assume an increasingly economic and physical character. It is therefore clear that anyone who wants to ensure himself a 'majority', in other words a number, will undergo the relevant conditioning, that is, he will have to restrict himself only to advancing the protection (even if dishonestly) of interests of this inferior type in his personal electoral program, or in his party's.

In the case of the democratic parliamentary system, we may add to this 'politicising', which, in the context of partisan politics, acquires many individual or social interests that in themselves should be non-political. Parties in the democratic system are not simple representatives of categories of interests. Tactically, they appear rather in a sort of contest or competition for the best defence of the interests of this or that group of voters. In reality, however, each of them has a political dimension, that is, each has its own political ideology. They do not recognise interests and considerations that transcend them, they participate in the 'empty state', and each one aims at the conquest of power, which leads to a totally chaotic and inorganic situation.

This political surplus value[152] of parties appears clearly in the liberal democratic thesis according to which the plurality of parties constitutes a guarantee for 'liberty'. Many contrasting opinions, many points of view, and 'debate' would allow us to choose the best direction without following orders. Naturally all this is nonsense, if in Parliament or, better, in the 'Chamber of Deputies', there is the same application of the numerical criterion of 'one man, one vote', so that the representatives each have an equal, single vote, like the citizens who elected them. Therefore, after the 'debate', the biggest number will always dominate, and in fact there will always be a minority that will submit to the purely numerical violence of the majority. But we also need to take into account the reality that the plurality of parties and points of view can be productive only in a context of advice and collaboration, that is, in a context that presupposes a unity of principle and goals, but not when every party has a political surplus value and its own ideology, and does not try to fulfil its own function in an organic and disciplined system, but rather 'attacks the stagecoach', that is, mounts an assault on the state in order to conquer power. In fact, there is continual talk today of 'political struggle' in no uncertain terms, a struggle in which, according to the rules of democracy, every means is good.

The fact is that we ought to distinguish between a representative system in general and a representative system that is egalitarian, which has a levelling effect on society and is based purely on number. The

---

152 'Surplus value' is a sarcastic reference to Marxist ideology, implying the Marxist basis of Italian *partitocrazia*.

state of the type that we call traditional recognised the representative principle, but in an organic context. It was a question not of representation or of individuals, but of 'bodies', where individuals were significant only insofar as they were part of a differentiated unity, and each individual had a different weight and quality. As a representation of bodies, the parliament, or another analogous institution, had an undoubted value, because it embraced the interests of the nation in all their richness and diversity. Thus, along with the representative principle, the hierarchical principle was affirmed, because the merely numerical force of the groups, bodies or partial unities that had their own representatives in parliament was not taken in account, but instead their function and dignity. The fact that the climate and values of a traditional state are different from a democracy's means that it automatically excludes the pre-eminence, which is imposed by number, of interests of a lower order, as takes place today and will always take place in the modern, absolute democracies, because mass parties will always necessarily prevail in them. The States-General, or parliament as it existed in Hungary and Austria, which was based on the plan of the *Ständestaat*,[153] a characteristic designation for the system of a unity where representation was qualitative, articulated and graded, was close to the structure we are alluding to. The corporations, the nobility, the scholars, the army, and so on were represented as bodies that corresponded to the nation, which was qualitatively differentiated so as to treat the interests of the nation and the public in concert.

[NOTE: It is worth noting that there was a system based on an articulation of the right to vote which existed for a long time in Prussia,[154] after the concession of universal suffrage. The electors were divided into three categories, and the weight of the vote of one category was not equal to that of another. In practical terms, the weight of the vote in each category was in inverse proportion to their respective numerical make-up.]

---

153 The term was used to describe a form of Catholic corporatist government that existed in Austria between the proclamation of the May Constitution of 1934 by Chancellor Engelbert Dollfuss, and lasted until the *Anschluss* of Austria with the Third Reich in 1938.

154 A three-class franchise system was set up in Prussia for elections following the Revolution of 1848. All men over the age of 24 could vote, and the three classes were divided up according to the amount of taxes paid by the individual. This system was abolished following the dissolution of the German Empire in 1918.

These considerations of principle, which we have developed to a certain extent, are necessary so that, by bringing ourselves in this regard
to a reality all too easily forgotten, we have the elements to evaluate
adequately what was positive in the attempt at a Fascist reform of the
system of representatives, a reform that can be described, depending on
one's point of view, as revolutionary or counterrevolutionary (counterrevolutionary, if we take into account the fact that the parliamentary
system, with its inorganic and quantitative basis, derived directly from
the revolutionary ideologies of 1789 and 1848). The Chamber of Fasces
and Corporations[155] signified in principle a return to the system of representation by 'bodies'. The direction taken can therefore be considered
as substantially positive.

There is, however, a difference, due to the accentuation of the aspect
of a representation of 'competences',[156] in rather technical terms, which
corresponded to the age. This emphasis, however, tended to categorically
eliminate what we have called the political or ideological surplus value
of representatives. Even with this restriction of the scope and concept
of 'bodies', which replaced political parties, there was clearly an overcoming of the absurd democratic electoral system, which could bring
to Parliament an incompetent party hack that nevertheless, by means
of compromises and backroom deals, could play a role in the cabinet as
a minister or undersecretary of state for a sector of national activity in
which he lacks any serious preparation and training, not to mention any
actual experience. The designation of parliamentary representation on
the basis of corporations and unions prevented this absurdity. It was not
the shapeless and ephemeral electoral mass, but its own circles of special-
ists who chose the representative as a person qualified for this function
and who was determined to be competent in his field.

Fascism, however, was also a mixed system in which designation
from above *per nomina*[157] was associated with election. Election or
designation by the 'body' concerned not a single person, but different
persons, among whom the government could choose, and in so doing

---

155 The Chamber of Fasces and Corporations was set up in January 1939 to replace
   the Chamber of Deputies. Unlike in the Chamber of Deputies, where representatives
   were chosen by popular vote, representatives in the new Chamber were nominated
   by the Fascist Grand Council, the National Council of Corporations, and the
   National Council of the Fascist Party.

156 'Competences' here refers to specialised areas of professional knowledge.

157 Latin: 'by appointment'.

could introduce criteria of a different order, even political criteria, without prejudice to the basic principle of the competences of the persons in question. Considered in this light, the Fascist reform therefore presented a character of rationality and plausibility. The actual praxis of the reform in the Fascist regime is another question, which concerns a field that, as we have said, falls outside the object of the present examination.

Therefore the Chamber of Fasces and Corporations was supposed to be a place, not of 'debates', but of coordinated labour, where criticism was admitted not on a political basis, but on a technical and objective one. Nevertheless, it was precisely this delimitation of scope inherent in representation by competences, with the inevitable emphasis that was placed on the productive economic sphere, which required an adequate institutional proclamation of the hierarchical principle in the sense of a higher request linked to the realm of ultimate ends. Once the parties were eliminated and representation was depoliticised, the purely political principle should have been concentrated and exercised on a distinct and superior level.

Even here, the state of a traditional type has often presented the model or outline of the system of two houses, with a lower house and an upper house. The closest example was the duality in England between the House of Commons and the House of Lords in its original form. A duality of this kind appears all the more necessary because Parliament was now, as we have said, composed of experts and corporations, and because organised 'bodies' that are exponents of higher values and traditions are practically non-existent in the modern world. Fascism found in Italy the duality of the Chamber of Deputies and the Senate.[158] The Fascist reform respected this duality, without investing the 'Upper House' with an adequately forceful reorganisation. During the Twenty Years, the Senate in general maintained its earlier character of an inefficient, decorative superstructure. A Senate with members designated exclusively from above, chosen in consideration especially for their political qualities, the quality of representatives of the 'transcendent' dimension of the state, and therefore also of spiritual, meta-economic and national factors, could have constituted a superior hierarchical presence in respect to the Chamber of Corporations. Wherever it became necessary, it could have asserted the 'order of ends', understood in the

158 In the Kingdom of Italy, senators were appointed by the King.

highest sense, before the 'order of means', and so established and realised the natural hierarchy of values and interests.

In this regard, however, Fascism's institutionally revolutionary and reconstructive force stopped halfway. In general, the Senate preserved the physiognomy given to it by tradition from the Italy of the late eighteenth and early nineteenth centuries, and so remained without a real function. Even in this respect, the negative influence of the pluralism of the institutions made itself felt: the Fascist Party's hierarchies, all the way to the Grand Council, were meant to have an especially political value, whereas there was also the legacy of the monarchical institutions of the earlier Italy, to which the old version of the Senate belonged. We could add the Royal Academy of Italy itself, insofar as it was supposed to bring together exponents of superior values in principle, but not to stay in the sphere of highbrow culture so as to render it useless. All this could have been reduced to what is essential, unified and reorganised, and here obviously we should refer to what we said about the establishment of an 'Order', which could have served as an essential nucleus within the Upper House. Despite all this, anyone who decides to make a comparison between the present Chamber of Deputies and especially the new Senate in Italy by considering them from the point of view of principles, in which, to a large extent, the absurd electoral principle of absolute democracy has been extended, should not have to hesitate, if he is asked to give his opinion concerning them.

Here and there in Fascism there appeared the aberrant formula of the 'state of labour', loudly proclaimed by the new constitution of the democratic state of Italy. Besides the concept of the 'ethical state' (the pedagogical state for spiritual minors), there were those who outlined the even more undesirable one of a 'humanism of labour' (here again we are talking about Giovanni Gentile). All this was merely the dross, the unessential and invalid parts of Fascism.

In fact, from the mouth of Mussolini himself, Fascism explicitly proclaimed, 'Corporations belong to the order of means and not to that of ends' (1934). The corporation is the institution with which 'the world of the economy, extraneous and disorganized until now, enters the state' (1934), thus allowing the political discipline to associate with the economic one. The entrance of the economy into the state should not be interpreted as introducing a 'Trojan horse'. Corporatism was not supposed to be a form or cover by means of which the economy would succeed in taking over the state, and so lead to the degradation and involution of the very idea of the state. The conclusion has effectively been the tendency of so-called 'pan-corporatism' expressed especially by some intellectuals of a Gentilian orientation at the corporative conference that was held at Ferrara in 1932. In this line there were those who could conceive of a type of corporative Communism ('proprietary corporatism' more or less under the control of the state) and who favoured the dissolution of the Party as an institution, to be replaced by a purely trade union/corporatist state. All these, however, remained ineffectual ideological dreams.

On the other hand, the distinction between the political sphere and the corporatist sphere was not abolished even in the opposite direction, starting from above, with a 'totalitarianism' imposed by the state. In fact, Mussolini indicated 'the totalitarian state' as third among the conditions for developing a 'full, complete, integral corporatism', along with ideal high tension and 'the introduction of political discipline along with economic discipline [...] so there may be, beyond the opposition of interests, a bond that unites everything'. He also declared, 'The corporatist economy has many forms and is harmonious. Fascism has never thought of reducing it all to a greatest common denominator, transforming all the nation's economies into a state monopoly. The corporations discipline them and the state does not take them over, except in the defence sector.' It was explicitly proclaimed that 'the corporatist state is not the economic state', which could be understood in a double sense: as opposition to the corporation's functioning either as the instrument of statist centralisation or as a takeover of the state by the economy.

IX

After this, we need to examine the corporatist principle in its economic and social aspect as well as the political one. In regard to this, too, Fascism restored, to a certain degree, a principle of the traditional legacy, the principle of the 'corporation' understood as an organic productive unity, not one fractured by the spirit of class and class struggle. In fact, the corporation as it existed in the context of artisan workmanship and before extreme industrialisation, and as it has often existed beginning with the best period of the Middle Ages (it is significant that abolishing the corporation was one of the first initiatives taken by the French Revolution), offered a plan that, adequately reorganised, could have served—and could still serve today—as a model for a general reconstructive action informed by the organic principle. Fascism, however, in fact performed this function only up to a certain point, mainly because of the remnants of the past that survived into the Twenty Years. Here we are dealing essentially with trade unionism, which continued to exercise a notable influence on Mussolini and the various elements close to him.

In its special aspect as an organisation that spans many businesses, the union movement is effectively inseparable from the concept of class struggle, and therefore also from the general Marxist view of society. This is a type of state within the state and therefore corresponds to one of the aspects of a system in which the authority of the state is minimised. The 'class' that is organised in the trade union is a part of the nation that aims at obtaining justice for itself, by itself, and which passes to direct action in terms that can often be defined as blackmail, in spite of the acknowledgement that it can extort: the so-called 'right to organise' is basically a right drawn from the sphere of effective rights that only the sovereign state ought to administer. It is known how for Sorel, whom Mussolini had admired in the past, trade unionism assumed a directly revolutionary value and was tied to a corresponding 'myth' or general idea of force.

On the other hand, we know that, in every regime that is not integrally socialist, such as those regimes where capitalism and private initiative have not been abolished, the existence of trade unionism brings about a situation that is chaotic, inorganic and unstable. Categories of workers struggle, using the instruments of the strike and other forms of blackmail, against the employers, who defend themselves with the 'lock-out', which has become increasingly ineffective and rare. The struggle deteriorates into one-sided pressure and extends to all contacts between workers and employers. Both groups care only for their own interests with no concern for the imbalances that their particular claims can cause to the nation as a whole, never mind the common good. The problem is usually dumped onto the state and the government, who therefore find themselves compelled to run back and forth knocking over and setting up the tottering and creaking structure over and over again. Only by believing in the miracle of some 'pre-established harmony', to use Leibniz's[159] expression, is it conceivable that the economy could function normally in a society where the state has increasingly given trade unions the right to organise themselves, and that the situation should not, as a result of numerous conflicts and other disruptions, become such that the only reasonable solution is to finally wipe the slate clean and accept the integrally socialist solution as the only one capable of establishing a principle of order and discipline, with a plan for the entire society. The situation of Italy at the moment in which we are writing can serve as a more than eloquent example of this truth.[160]

With corporatism, Fascism therefore undertook to overcome the state of affairs we have discussed as created by the union movement and the class struggle. It was a question of re-establishing the unity of various elements of productive activity, a unity prejudiced on the one hand by the deviations and prevarications of late capitalism, and on the other by the Marxist intoxication that was widespread throughout the working class masses, by excluding the socialist solution and reaffirming

---

159 Leibniz, Gottfried Wilhelm (1646-1716) was a highly influential German mathematician and philosopher. According to him, the universe consists of substances he termed 'monads'. All monads are independent from one another, but seem to interact without problems because God has set all of them to harmonise with all the others. He discusses this at length in his work *The Monadology*.

160 In 1970, at the time Evola was preparing the second edition of this book, Italy was undergoing a great deal of unrest in the form of labour strikes, student protests, and the 'Years of Lead', which saw a wave of bombings, shootings and assassinations carried out by radicals of both the Left and the Right.

instead the authority of the state as the regulator and guardian of the idea of justice on the economic and social level. But, as we said, this reform, which was inspired by an organic principle and led to Fascist corporatism and its corresponding praxis, stopped halfway and did not reach the roots of the evil, because the Fascism of the Twenty Years lacked the courage to assume a clearly anti-union position. Instead, the system passed laws that resulted in confirming the division of employers and workers into two groups. This duality was not overcome where it ought to have been, that is, in the businesses themselves, by means of a new organic structuring, (that is, in its 'infrastructure'). Instead a general state superstructure was constructed, which was affected by a heavy centralism that was bureaucratic and, in practice, often parasitic and inefficient. Granted, Fascism eliminated the most disastrous aspects of the earlier system by prohibiting strikes and the 'lockout' and establishing regulations for labour contracts and forms of control that obviated what we have called the 'anarchism of claims' from every sector. Still, it was always a question of external regulations, at the most like an umpire's, which did not develop inside the concrete life of the community. Nevertheless, as we have seen, Mussolini, by pointing out the way towards an ideal special tension and emphasizing that the character of the corporation was not only economic but also ethical, demonstrated an accurate sense of the point at which the corporatist reforms should arrive. The essential point was a new climate that acted in a direct and formative way on businesses and restored to them the traditional character of 'corporations'. It therefore first dealt with acting on the mentalities of those involved. On the one hand, it was necessary to eliminate the proletarian and Marxist influences on the worker, and on the other to destroy the purely 'capitalist' mentality of the entrepreneur.

We might mention that, in principle, it was rather German National Socialism, and also the counterrevolutionary movements in Spain (Falangism) and Portugal (Salazar's constitution) that proceeded more decisively ahead in the correct, traditional direction. In the German case, even in this regard one should think of the influence exercised by the survival of older structures supported by a corresponding attitude and a corresponding tradition that did not exist in Italy. It was this influence that was bound to continue even after the collapse of Hitlerism and the formal elimination of National Socialist labour legislation, and it was due to this influence that what has been called the 'economic miracle',[161] the rapid rise of West Germany after the great catastrophe, took place.

National Socialism disbanded the unions and—as we shall say in our *Notes on the Third Reich*—aimed at overcoming the class struggle with a corresponding dualism right *inside* the business, within *every* single substantial business, along with giving it an organic and hierarchical formation to encourage a strict cooperation, and so reproducing in the business the same plan that the regime had proposed for the state. Once the enterprise was thought of in terms of a 'community' (that could be considered as corresponding to that of the ancient corporation), it became possible to recognize in the head of the business, by means of an analogy, the function of a *Führer*, with the title of *Betriebsführer* ('*Führer* of the business'), while the workers came to be called his *Gefolgschaft*, a term that means literally his 'retinue', that is, a whole composed of associated elements that were supposed to be united by a sentiment of solidarity, hierarchical subordination and loyalty. This 'reciprocity of rights and duties', which according to the Fascist Charter of Labour (paragraph 7)[162] was supposed to derive from the 'cooperation of productive forces', came to be transferred to something living that alone could give it a solid foundation. It could be said that, against the Marxist and materialist mentality, the same type of 'military' attitude in the general sense, of which we have spoken earlier, could be made equally effective on the level of work and production.

In Germany the roles of mediating and reconciling disputes remained within the firm, with the recognition of the political principle as the final arbiter. These tasks, which in Italy were entrusted to the state Fascist corporative organs, were supposed to be discharged on an adequate scale in Germany by political trustees who were not part of the businesses,

---

161 The 'economic miracle' was the rapid recovery of the West German economy following the devastation of the Second World War, beginning in 1948 and lasting into the 1950s.

162 The Fascist Charter of Labour was enacted in 1927. Paragraph 7 reads: 'The Corporate State considers private initiative in the field of production the most efficacious and most useful instrument in the interest of the nation. Private organization of production being a function of national interest, the organization of the enterprise is responsible to the State for the direction of its production. Reciprocity of the rights and duties is derived from the collaboration of the productive forces. The technician, office employee and worker is an active collaborator in the economic undertaking, the direction of which is the right of the employer, who has the responsibility for it.' The complete text of the Charter is available at webdev.archive.org/stream/FascistLaborCharter/LaborCharter djvu.txt.

and who had the power to settle disputes, make recommendations and eventually modify the agreed-upon regulations by appealing to superior principles. The very designation of the highest court of this system as the 'Social Honour Court',[163] *Soziales Ehrengericht*, emphasises again the ethical aspect that was supposed to regulate solidarity between the workers and the owners within every business. As in the Fascist system, the principle of the German system was, in a word, that the entrepreneur's free initiative was accompanied by a responsibility before the state for directing production. Here we can recall once more the considerations we have already mentioned in regard to anti-totalitarianism and decentralisation: liberty and free initiative can be conceded to a greater degree, the greater the central power and the greater the gravitational centre to which the parts are connected by an immaterial, ethical link, more than through any kind of contractual or binding positive norm. In Germany's case, the businesses in their new form as corporative bodies were only united under the auspices of the so-called 'German Labour Front'.

We can mention that Spain moved in a similar direction of organic, intra-company reconstruction. Also in Spain, employers and workers were not opposed to each other in a kind of permanent cold war, but were united by hierarchical solidarity. In the original plan of the so-called 'vertical corporation', the entrepreneur assumed the character of a leader—the *jefe de empresa*.[164] He had with him the *jurados de empresa*[165] as an advisory organ, corresponding perhaps to internal commissions and also to unions as they existed at one time in the United States (unions for each business or industrial complex, not organisations for all businesses of the same type). The system emphasised a principle of collaboration and loyalty instead of just defending the workers' interests.

It is appropriate to consider briefly the developments that the second Fascism, the republican and 'social' fascism of Salò, tried to give to the corporative reform. There are various aspects to this issue. In fact, on one hand, we can think of real progress made in the direction we have just discussed, because special attention was given to the figure of the business leader and, in principle, the projected establishment in the businesses of

---

163 The Social Honour Courts were established to mediate between the workers and the business owners in factories. Although modified by them, this was actually not an innovation of the National Socialists, as similar courts had existed in Germany prior to the Third Reich.

164 Spanish: 'manager of a company'.

165 Spanish: 'company juries'.

joint 'management committees' could naturally have been oriented in the direction of a regime of organic cooperation in fields where it would not be absurd to consult a layman (like particularly specialised technical problems or those involving upper management). The most audacious and revolutionary trait, however, was the so-called Verona Manifesto,[166] which was an attack on parasitic capitalism. The increased dignity and authority of the business leader that we just mentioned was acknowledged only in one who was 'the first worker', that is, to the committed capitalist entrepreneur, and not to the capitalist speculator who was foreign to the productive process and simply the beneficiary of dividends. (Marxist polemic can be justified, at least in part, only in regard to this second type.) In regard to this, too, we can think of a revival of the model of the ancient corporation, where the 'capitalists' who owned the means of production were not an element foreign to or separate from production, but was engaged in it as masters of the craft.

But the negative counterpart of this labour legislation of the second Fascism is visible in two points. The first concerns the so-called 'socialisation' with which, even if it perhaps started from an organic exigency, overshot the mark and revealed a demagogic tendency—which, however, we cannot rule out was indulged in because of tactical considerations prompted by the critical, not to say desperate, situation in which the Fascism of Salò found itself. Mussolini was perhaps looking for ways to attract the working class, which was irresistibly drawn toward the orbit of Leftist ideologies. We could thus speak of an attempted opening, understood as a means of stopping the true Left. Socialisation in itself, however, could only represent an attack on business from the bottom and, aside from the absurdity of such a technical and functional order, on which it is not appropriate to linger, it is clear that it did not respond to the actual legitimate situation that inspired it, because of its evident one-sidedness.

In fact, the principal suggestion of the system proposed by this aspect of republican Fascist legislation concerns the sharing of blue- and white-collar workers in the enterprise's profits, something that in itself, within given limits, could be a just limitation of the possibilities left to a capitalism that exploits and accumulates profits. But regarding the elimination of these appealing aspects of the system, it would be enough to

---

166 The Verona Manifesto was issued by the government of the Italian Social Republic in November 1943, being its only major statement of policy. It was strongly socialist and pro-labour in orientation.

emphasise that, if we wanted to create a regime of true solidarity, sharing in the profits would have to have as its natural counterpart the sharing also of the eventual losses by the masses, with a corresponding reduction in wages and stipends, meaning solidarity in good fortune as well as bad, which in itself would be enough to cool enthusiasm for such a plan. The proper solution, which would be capable of ensuring a true commitment and shared responsibility, would have been not 'socialisation', but rather a system of blue- and white-collar workers receiving a percentage of the company's stocks (which would be inalienable to avoid speculation as dividends rose and fell), but not so large as to interfere with the entrepreneur's ownership of the business. This system has recently been tried experimentally by certain big businesses abroad. This is certainly not the place, however, to examine problems of this sort, which we have mentioned only to show, by means of a comparison, the limits and compromises of the labour legislation of the second Fascism.

The second negative and regressive point in this legislation was the strengthening of the union movement and, at the same time, centralisation by creating a single confederation in which the leadership would have been given to the unions, which were still acknowledged and tolerated, who would then have had the task of deciding 'in all questions relevant to the life of the business and the direction and development of production in the context of the national plan established by competent state organs'. In a different sense from what was part of the dualistic plan of corporative legislation during the Twenty Years, the confederation of the second Fascism did not contemplate separate groupings for entrepreneurs and workers, but instead aimed at an 'umbrella of a single confederation comprising all workers, technicians, and professionals'.[167] Before this bloc, the second Fascism obviously treated as secondary the problem—which is fundamental for us—of the organic reconstruction of infrastructure in every business, considered in its autonomy. We can then see again in outline, on the national and governmental level, an ambiguity that in principle could create either of the two negative developments we have pointed out earlier: the takeover of the state by the economy: 'labour' and production, on the one hand, or, on the other, the

---

167 Article 16 of the Verona Manifesto read, in part, 'All the trade unions are gathered together under the umbrella of a single confederation comprising all workers, technicians, and professionals (but excluding landlords, who are neither managers nor technicians.' From Jeffrey Schnapp, Maria Stampino & Olivia Sears (eds.), *A Primer of Italian Fascism* (Lincoln, NE: University of Nebraska Press, 2000), p. 201.

'totalitarian' nationalisation of the economy. If the formula we have just quoted, which spoke of 'a national plan established by competent organs of the state', could lead in the other direction, perhaps we should mention that the 'bloc' considered in that way could also enter into the vision of 'total mobilisation' imposed by an emergency situation, and could be justified by that situation alone (and for the duration of the emergency). This was exactly the situation in which 'republican' Fascism found itself in the tragic climate at the end of the war. Clearly, however, this enters into the field of contingency, from which it is impermissible to gather anything that concerns the areas of doctrine or of normative principles.

Concluding our overall examination of the Fascist corporatist experiment, we can therefore see that all sorts of claims were made, the validity and legitimacy of which become clearer when we remember the present economic and social situation, and when we acknowledge the critical and chaotic aspects that remain despite certain outward signs of economic recovery, or even of an ephemeral prosperity. These include, for instance, the exacerbation of the class struggle and the progressive yielding of the state before a legalised demagoguery that now seems to know no limits. Again, we should note and highlight that the positive elements of Fascism in this area, as well as whatever further reconstructive developments could have taken place with the removal of the limitations we have mentioned, do not amount to anything 'revolutionary' in the negative or exclusively innovatory sense, but, once more, relate only to elements within Fascism for which the proper soil was an older culture: elements of traditional inspiration, whether or not the promoters of corporative Fascism were conscious of them.

As the reader will have seen, we have not thought it appropriate to speak at all about 'national socialism', in which some have wanted to see one of the essential and valid traits of Fascism: the creation of this kind of socialism, in their opinion, was supposed to have been the principal mission assumed not only in Italy but also in Germany, and the Fascist Charter of Labour was supposed to have laid the foundations for this special 'socialist culture'. We cannot take these, and similar, ideas seriously. We refuse to discuss 'socialism' apart from its values, which are incompatible with Fascism's highest and clearly asserted vocation. Socialism is socialism, and adding the adjective 'national' merely disguises it as a 'Trojan horse'. Once 'national socialism' was established (with the inevitable elimination of the values and hierarchies incompatible with it) it would soon become socialism without an adjective, because you cannot stop halfway down a slope.

In its day, Italian Fascism was one of the most advanced and progressive regimes in its social measures. The corporatism of the Twenty Years, in terms of what was valid in it, should be interpreted in the context of an organic and anti-Marxist idea, and therefore outside of everything that can be legitimately called 'socialism'. Exactly—but only—to this extent could Fascism have been a 'third way',[168] a possibility offered to European civilisation, opposed to both Communism and capitalism. Therefore, every interpretation of Fascism as an 'opening to the Left' ought to be avoided, if one wants to avoid degrading it. With all due respect for some enthusiasts of the 'national state of labour' who seem today not to have noticed that while they would like to play the role of opposition and even be 'revolutionaries', this is more or less exactly the institutional formula proclaimed in the constitution of today's democratic and anti-Fascist Italy.

---

168 Proponents of fascism, both in Italy and other countries, talked of it as the only alternative to democracy and Marxism. Mussolini said of the Second World War in 1940, 'This conflict must not be allowed to cancel out all our achievements of the past eighteen years, nor, more importantly, extinguish the hope of a Third Alternative held out by Fascism to mankind fettered between the pillar of capitalist slavery and the post of Marxist chaos.' Quoted in Frank Joseph, *Mussolini's War: Fascist Italy's Military Struggles from Africa and Western Europe to the Mediterranean and Soviet Union 1935-45* (West Midlands, UK: Helion & Company, 2010), p. 50.

X

Let us proceed to another point, concerning the national economy in terms of its relationship to the international economy. In many circles today, it is fashionable to condemn the Fascist principle of autarchy as an absurdity. From our point of view, we cannot be in complete agreement with this opinion.

Just as when we are dealing with persons, so with nations, one of the greatest goods is liberty and autonomy. Mussolini affirmed this need clearly when he said, 'Without economic independence the political independence of a nation is doubtful, and a nation of great military power may become the victim of an economic blockade'[169] (1937). Therefore, in Mussolini's opinion, the new phase of Italian history ought 'to be dominated by this postulate: to realise the greatest possible degree of autonomy in the economic life of the nation in the shortest time possible' (1936). Talk about a 'mysticism of autarchy' is a natural part of the abuse in recent times of the term 'mysticism'. [NOTE: We find the same abuse in the expression 'Fascist mysticism'. There was even a 'School of Fascist Mysticism' created at Milan.[170] Although this organisation promoted some interesting initiatives and involved various qualified individuals from the new generation of those days, there was certainly no reason to talk about 'mysticism'. The most one could legitimately refer to prior to this development was an 'ethic of Fascism'. As we have said, Fascism did not confront the problem of higher values, of the sacred, which are the only values in relation to which we can talk about 'mysticism'. In regard to these values, however, during the Twenty Years, Fascism remained on the level of vague and conformist references to the dominant religion.] We can, however, speak perfectly well of an 'ethic of autarchy', on the basis of the word's origin. Autarchy comes to us from Classical antiquity,

---

169 Quoted in Cesare Santoro, *Hitler Germany as Seen by a Foreigner* (Berlin: Internationaler Verlag, 1939), p. 85.

170 The School of Fascist Mysticism was established in 1930 with the intention of establishing the basis for a mystical basis for the Fascist community, based upon the idea of fideism, or an irrationalist conception of faith.

especially from the Stoic[171] schools that professed an ethics of independence or the sovereignty of the individual. In order to guard this value, where it was necessary, one had to follow the strict principle of *abstine et sustine*.[172]

The Fascist principle of autarchy can therefore be considered as a kind of extension of this ethic to the plane of the national economy. An orientation of which we can completely approve is that of, if necessary, holding the general standard of living relatively low, adopting what the English call 'austerity', which, even in a different context, has had to be practiced here and there by different nations after the Second World War, but assuring ourselves a maximum of independence. In the case of a nation with limited natural resources, like Italy, a certain regime of autarchy and austerity was, in fact, the right direction. As for the course of the national life, we hold the normal situation to be the complete opposite of everything we are witnessing today: apparently generalised prosperity and thoughtless living from day to day beyond one's means, along with a frightening state debt balance, leading to extreme economic and social instability, growing inflation and an invasion of foreign capital which brings with it many important visible and invisible influences.

Naturally, it is not right to go overboard in the opposite direction. In every respect, we can be guided by the analogy offered by the behaviour of a man worthy of the name. He can promote the development of his body and bodily health, but not become its slave. When it is necessary, he reins in the corresponding impulses and makes them obey a higher will, even at the cost of sacrifices. He does the same thing every time he wants to or must confront tasks that demand particular strain. In order to make possible what, on the national level, corresponds to a similar line, adequate relations have to be established between the political principle of an organic national state and the world of the economy, which corresponds to its corporal part.

In Fascism, on the one hand, the creation of a strong state was envisioned in which all the possibilities of the nation were activated, but it cannot be denied, on the other hand, that by autarchy Fascism did not

---

171 Stoicism was a school of philosophy which originated in Classical Athens, although as a term it continues to be applied today to philosophies which share its general characteristics. Basically, the Stoics believed that it is human emotions which lead individuals into error, and that the only way to lead a truly virtuous life is to transcend the emotions. They also emphasized the importance of logic and reason as the sole paths to genuine knowledge.

172 Latin: 'abstain and sustain'.

envision a sort of 'splendid isolation' (as the French say) of the nation, rendered self-sufficient as far as possible. It was also preparing and collecting the nation's forces in anticipation of an armed encounter between states, with the experiences of the campaign in Ethiopia[173] serving as a warning. Mussolini's statements quoted above also undeniably emphasise this aspect. Still, apart from all this, and understanding the principle of autarchy in terms of a challenge to the economy and its presumed iron laws that create 'our destiny', it cannot be said in this regard that the results of experience have been negative. In Italy and also in Germany before the Second World War, internal economic affairs could go on more or less as usual despite the virtual international boycott suffered by the two nations and, especially, the devaluing of their currency abroad.

So from autarchy as scandal and economic heresy, we can move on to considerations of a more general character.

The Marxist formula 'the economy is our destiny',[174] with the corresponding interpretation of history as a function of the economy, is well-known. But economic determinism has also been acknowledged by currents other than Marxism, some of which are even opposed to it. Here we can say that, if taken in itself, this formula is absurd, but unfortunately not if we take into consideration the modern world, because the modern world has caused it to become a reality to an increasingly greater degree. The pure *homo oeconomicus*[175] is an abstraction but, like many abstractions, it can become a reality by means of a process of hypertrophy and the absolutising of one part in respect to the whole. At the point in which the economic interest becomes dominant, it is natural that man becomes the subject of the laws of the economy, which acquire an almost autonomous character, until other interests are reaffirmed and a superior power intervenes.

---

173 Conflict between Italy and Ethiopia dated back to Italy's colonial interests in the country during the nineteenth century. Following a crisis, Italy attacked Ethiopia in October 1935. Although the Italians ultimately won in May 1936, their poor performance against the Ethiopians showed the weakness and unpreparedness of the Italian military, and it also isolated Italy from the international community, which reacted with condemnation. Italy's possession of Ethiopia only lasted for four years, as they were driven from the country by the British in 1940, during the Second World War.

174 This phrase was first used by Walther Rathenau, the German Foreign Minister, in 1922. He was assassinated by the Freikorps in 1922. Rathenau was not a Marxist.

175 Latin: 'economic man'.

That 'economic man' did not exist was also Mussolini's point of view, who opposed his idea of 'integral man' (1933) to 'economic man'.[176] His idea was that 'politics has dominated and will always dominate the economy', mentioning in this context that what gets conceived as man's destiny 'is, at least three quarters of it, created by weakness or strength of will' (1932). Here we can mention Spengler's perspectives. In his examination of the forms with which a cycle of cultures comes to an end, with the descent to the level of a *Zivilisation*, he considered the level at which the economy becomes dominant and creates a certain connection between democracy, capitalism and finance. This connection demonstrates, moreover, the illusory nature of the 'liberty' claimed in this last period. Obviously 'political liberties' are nothing without economic liberty or autonomy, in the individual field as well as the collective one: in the collective field because it is the groups in possession of wealth who control the press and all the other means of shaping 'public opinion' and disseminating propaganda in a democratic regime; in the individual and practical field, because access to the various 'conquests' of modern technical and economic civilisation, with its apparent prosperity, are paid for with just as many constraints on the individual, with an increasingly rigorous integration into the collective gears set in motion by the economy and in front of which 'political liberties' are something derisory.

Spengler, however, predicted a successive phase, which he called the phase of 'absolute politics' and which was related to the appearance of those new leaders of a problematic type, of which we have spoken earlier (cf. Chapter VII). While we hold to the reservations we have made concerning this last subject, from the perspective of the whole it is, however, possible to imagine a change in the situation so as to create a strong state, based on the detached principle of authority. The strong state can be given the task of reining in the 'blind giant'[177] of the economy as destiny. Werner Sombart[178] coined the expression 'blind giant' with

---

176 Mussolini said, 'We have rejected the theory of the economic man, the Liberal theory, and we are, at the same time, emancipated from what we have heard said about work being a business. The economic man does not exist; the integral man, who is political, who is economic, who is religious, who is holy, who is combative, does exist.' Quoted in George Seldes, *Sawdust Caesar: The Untold History of Mussolini and Fascism* (London: Barker, 1936), p. 426.

177 Werner Sombart refers to capitalism by this term in his book *The Quintessence of Capitalism* (New York: E. P. Dutton & Co., 1915), p. 359.

178 Werner Sombart (1863-1941) was a German economist and sociologist, who came to support the idea of 'German socialism' late in his life.

reference especially to high capitalism and its immanent determinisms. This specific reference can be taken into consideration: beginning with the principle of the pre-eminence of politics over the economy, and with a return to the idea of the true state. With its sovereignty and authority realised in a system of adequate social structures, even the monstrous development of capitalism in the direction of unfettered productivity can be limited, with the ultimate end of restoring the economy, and everything that is economic, to the subordinate position in which it becomes only a means to an end, and a circumscribed dominion within a much vaster hierarchy of values and interests.

To complete these considerations, it is possible to specify this ultimate end in regard to its content, and say that, from our point of view, the essential thing would be to reach an equilibrium, a stability, and put a stop to unlimited change. There could be no question of this in Fascism, which still had before it the hard work of getting the nation into economic, industrial and social shape. This was enough of a task, even apart from its expansionist projects which were tied to a certain aspiration toward 'greatness', rather than to the 'splendid isolation' of autarchy, as we have called it. Under these conditions, an active and dynamic orientation was only natural, a drive forward. The formula 'anyone who stops is lost' could even be enunciated, despite its problematic character, indicating the obviously anti-autarchic implications of accepting one's entrance into a general process of conditioning without defensive measures.

So no one asked the ultimate question, namely that of the ideal culture to strive for, definitely or in principle. That would mean wondering how far we felt ourselves called to go against the current of the general movement that was carrying the modern world towards what was predicted to be progress but, in relation to its genuine internal sense, should rather be called, as by Bernanos,[179] a 'retreat forward'. How far, at a particular time, would it be appropriate to consider an orientation that could be called 'opposition to progress' by people who confuse stability and a willed, positive limit with immobility and inertia, and who do not acknowledge that stopping, a break on the 'horizontal' direction, the direction of change and evolution in a material, technical and economic sense of processes that end by escaping from man's control. This will

---

179 Georges Bernanos (1888-1948) was a French writer who was anti-democratic in his beliefs.

always be the precondition for progress or movement in a 'vertical' direction, for the realisation of higher possibilities and the true autonomy of the person, and finally, to use a well-known formula, for a realisation of 'being' beyond 'well-being'.

All this obviously carries us rather far beyond the topic of an examination of the doctrine of Fascism, except for the possibilities that are virtually offered by the relationship between political power and the economy that were conceived and in part realised by Fascism. For these possibilities to succeed we must presuppose an adequate choice of vocations and, naturally and essentially, the eventual stabilising within the nation of a certain general climate and a different vision of life, which are opposed to those that are in fact coming irresistibly to predominate in our time.

XI

Even among those in Italy today who criticise the democratic regime and do not deny the value of some aspects of Fascism, 'racism' has been judged, in general, to be one of the dark aspects of Fascism about which it is better to keep silent, or as a kind of 'foreign body' that wormed its way into the system. In this interpretation, Fascism is supposed to be the subordinate and imitator of Hitlerism in the last period of the Italian-German alliance, the Rome-Berlin Axis.[180]

In this way of thinking, a significant role has often been played by the ambiguity resulting from making 'racism' a simple synonym for anti-Semitism and the brutal persecution of the Hebrew. So it can happen that a journal that calls itself 'neo-Fascist' highlighted various data gathered even from Hebrew authors in order to rub out the alleged stain and demonstrate that Mussolini was not really 'racist', because during the war, in the most critical period of the German occupation of Italy, Fascism not only did not persecute the Jews, but often even protected them. On this subject there is an obvious confusion between what could be attributed to humanitarian sentiment and an aversion for certain deplorable methods used by the Germans, and a question of principle.

So it will be appropriate to offer a brief exposition of the subject. We can speak of three factors that led Mussolini to confront the problem of race in 1938.[181] On 5 August 1938, an official document[182] declared, 'The climate is now ripe for an Italian racism', for which the Grand Council outlined the fundamental directives the following October. The first legislative provisions 'for the defence of the Italian race' were

---

180 The Rome-Berlin Axis was established on 22 May 1939 by the signing of the 'Pact of Steel', in which the two nations pledged to come to the aid of the other in the event of war.

181 Prior to the issuing of the 'Manifesto of Race' in July 1938, the Fascist regime had had no official racial doctrine.

182 This was announced in the first issue of the Fascist publication *La Difesa della Razza*, which was published on that date. *La Difesa* was intended to inspire popular support for Fascism's new racial policies.

promulgated the following month. Of the three factors, the one that concerned the Hebraic problem was the most incidental. There are few or no references to this problem in Mussolini's early writings. One can only cite an old article that mentions a well-known theme, that the Hebrew, subjugated and deprived of the usual means to compete directly in the modern world, had recourse to the indirect means constituted by money, finance and intelligence (in the profane sense) to exercise power and for self-affirmation. In addition, in an article from 1919, Mussolini wondered whether Bolshevism, which was supported in its origins by Jewish bankers in London and New York and counted (at that time) numerous Hebrews among its leaders, did not represent 'Israel's revenge against the Aryan race'.[183]

On the other hand, there is no need to recall that anti-Semitism was certainly not born with Nazism, and that the Hebrew throughout history, beginning with the Roman world, has been the subject of aversion and persecution. In the Christian era this has often been sanctioned by sovereigns, popes and councils. Moreover, it must be acknowledged that the Jewish problem in Italy was never a particularly hot issue, and Mussolini's stance towards it in 1938 had a more political than ideological character. In fact, there had been a notable increase in reports by Italian diplomats and other sources of information about the growth of militant anti-Fascist hostility demonstrated by Jewish elements abroad, especially in America, that was connected (or not) with Italy's alliance with Germany. So Mussolini was finally compelled to react, and the Jews in Italy, who, apart from a few exceptions, had not given any special indications of anti-Fascist sentiments (there were Jews among the *squadristi*, the Fascist toughs) ended up suffering the consequences of the attitude of their non-Italian co-religionists because of measures that, however, can in no way be compared with the German ones, and very often remained on paper and were not enforced. Since we are discussing doctrine here, we do not have to deal with this aspect of Fascist 'racism'. An examination of the Jewish problem in its full complexity belongs to a different context.[184]

---

183 Mussolini wrote this in his 'Il Popolo d'Italia', quoted in Michele Sarfatti, *The Jews in Mussolini's Italy: From Equality to Persecution* (Madison, WI: University of Wisconsin Press, 2006), p. 42.

184 See Julius Evola, *Three Aspects of the Jewish Problem* (Kemper, France: Thompkins & Cariou, 2003).

As for 'race', Mussolini often talked about it. At a time when there can have been no suspicion of Hitler's influence, in April 1921, Mussolini delivered a speech in Bologna which connected the birth of Fascism to 'a profound, perennial need of our Aryan and Mediterranean stock, that at a certain moment felt itself threatened in its essential reasons for existence'. From the same year comes his affirmation that 'it is with the race that history is made' and in 1927 he stated, 'We must rigorously watch over the destiny of the race; we must take care of the race'.[185] Many other, similar references can be given. In 1938, at the general congress of the Fascist Party, Mussolini could recall these precise antecedents in rejecting the accusation of simply aping the Germans, adding also that when he had talked of stock, he meant 'to refer to race'. If, however, in the first quotation, the term 'Aryan' could have a specifically racist meaning, in all the other cases he talked about race in a general sense. In fact, we often encounter a definite confusion between the concepts of race and nation. This kind of confusion continues to appear in the so-called 'Manifesto of Race'[186] (a thoroughly botched and superficial document), which talks of the 'Italian race'. The same expression is used in the Fascist 'racist' legislation of 1938. Naturally, this is absurd. No historical nation is a 'race'. Apart from some eugenicist examples, talk about the 'defence of the race' in these terms ends up giving a vague pseudo-biological and ethnic flourish to the nationalist position. At most, the words could be referring to an 'historical ethnic stock'. It is not enough. We should point out that identifying a race with a nation, and exalting what was supposed to find its main expression in the National Socialist collectivising concept of the *Volksgemeinschaft* (that is, the national and racial unity, or community of the race/people) ends with attacking the notion of race itself, emptying it of all meaning by democratising it. As K. A. Rohan[187] has correctly noted, there was still one thing that democracy had not been able to conquer, that is, race in the aristocratic

---

185 Mussolini said this in his Ascension Day speech of 26 May 1927, quoted in R. J. B. Bosworth, *Mussolini's Italy: Life Under the Fascist Dictatorship, 1915-1945* (New York: Penguin Books, 2007).

186 'The Manifesto of Race' is included in *A Primer of Italian Fascism*.

187 Prince Karl Anton Rohan (1898-1975) was an Austrian First World War veteran, monarchist and anti-modernist who later supported both Fascism and National Socialism, and hoped for a reconciliation between Christianity and the latter. He published his own *European Review* from 1925 until 1936, which called for the creation of a new European identity in keeping with Europe's unique cultural and religious mission, and which would revive Europe's ancient values.

sense, because only an *elite* is 'thoroughbred'[188] and a 'race', while the people is only people, a mass. With a promiscuous identification of race with nation to the point of speaking of an 'Italian race', a 'German race', and so on, this last bulwark falls and collapses. So we could and still can take a position against this kind of 'racism' by assuming an aristocratic and hierarchical point of view.[189]

In any case, the second factor that led to Fascism's racist orientation was the concept of a type of national 'racial' consciousness. This concept is also linked to an accidental circumstance, the conquest of Ethiopia and the creation of the African empire. In this regard, Fascist 'racism' had the same practical and non-ideological character of the attitudes that were shared by many European nations with colonies, with England at the forefront, which nourished a sentiment of 'race' in order to protect the prestige of Whites with adequate measures against coloured peoples, and to prevent miscegenation, which would lead to bastard and hybrid crossbreeding. This was more or less the meaning of a decree promulgated by the Fascist government as early as 1937.[190] Mussolini therefore did nothing more than follow what was already traditional before the rise of the democratic ideology, with its principle of the so-called 'self-determination of peoples', which was proclaimed by Whites, and then boomeranged against them, provoking the emergence, demands and uprising of coloured peoples, until the Europeans themselves became infected with the psychosis of anti-colonialism.

Mussolini, on the other hand, had acknowledged the 'fertilising, beneficent and unassailable inequality of men',[191] and his conduct was therefore, in this regard, coherent, and, from our point of view, correct. Distances had to be maintained. The next step could be seen in what he said in a speech on 18 September 1938, when he spoke of the necessity of arousing in Italians 'a clear, severe consciousness of race that would establish not only differences, but also very clear superiorities'. It is appropriate, however, to remember that in another, earlier speech,

---

188 In Evola's Italian, this reads as *essere di razza*. According to Spengler and other authors, one who is 'of race' represents the highest qualities of a particular people. This elite, therefore, are the only genuine representatives of a people.

189 See Julius Evola, *The Elements of Racial Education* (Kemper, France: Thompkins & Cariou, 2005).

190 This was the year that the first law against race-mixing was introduced in occupied Ethiopia. A similar law had already been enacted in Eritrea in 1933.

191 Mussolini, 'The Doctrine of Fascism'.

delivered to Eastern students, Mussolini had taken a position against inferior and materialist colonialism, condemning the attitude of those who thought of their colonial territories only in terms of 'sources of raw materials and markets for factory-made goods'. Thus he drew close to the fundamental point. Beyond all prejudice linked simply to skin colour, it was necessary to establish a hierarchical principle, and confront the problem of the legitimacy of the right to rule over a people and their commensurate culture. It is not possible to hide the serious character of this problem. In fact, if we consider the period of true colonialism, we have to acknowledge that this legitimacy was largely non-existent, when it was not a question of savages, Negroes, and other inferior races, but also of peoples that already possessed their own ancient civilisation and tradition, like, for instance, the case of the Hindus. To these peoples, 'Whites' could present nothing besides their technological civilisation and their material and organisational superiority, along with Christianity and its strange claim to be the only true religion or, at least, the highest religion. They confronted the serious implications of the hierarchical principle and the invocation of 'race consciousness' (the race/nation) insofar as the latter ought to include a sentiment not only of differences, but also of a real superiority. It is clear that we cannot take into account here the problems of a 'people without room',[192] possibly exasperated by a 'demographic campaign', and we have already pointed this out in speaking of the last issue. The pressure of numbers cannot make any Right meaningful in a higher, ethical or spiritual sense, and Mussolini's famous apostrophe at the time of the campaign in Ethiopia, 'Proletarian and Fascist Italy, on your feet!' was certainly one of the most deplorable ever suggested by the 'populist' component of his personality. At most, he could have spoken of an Italy of workers, without borrowing the Marxist jargon and transferring, as it were, the corresponding, fatal myth of the 'class struggle' (something Corradini[193] had already started to do in a nationalist tone) to the international sphere.

Then again, there is no need to say that, in the condition to which the Western peoples have been reduced today, problems of the sort we

---

192 'People without room' was a phrase coined by the German nationalist writer Hans Grimm, and which expressed his belief that lack of geographical space was hampering the development of the German nation. This phrase became a popular National Socialist slogan, and was used to justify German expansionism into Eastern Europe and Russia.

193 Enrico Corradini (1865-1931) was an Italian writer who was the leader of the Italian Nationalist Association.

were just now discussing have become devoid of all sense. On the one hand, today there subsists only concealed forms of economic colonialism, that is, the influence upon the 'underdeveloped' coloured peoples who have finally become independent by means of foreign capital and industry (this is the so-called 'second colonialism', in which America and Russia are the principal rivals).[194] On the other hand, there is an increasingly clear renunciation of real independence in the new non-European 'nations' because we are facing a strange paradox: apart from primitive and genuinely inferior ethnic stocks, a series of non-European peoples have broken free of the 'colonialist' yoke only to submit to it in a worse form than previously existed in the straightforward economic exploitation administered by foreigners. Increasingly renouncing their traditions, which date back for ages, these peoples have Westernised, adopting the culture, ideologies, political forms and lifestyles of White peoples, therefore increasingly capitulating to the pseudo-civilisation of Whites, with no other ambition than 'development' and self-affirmation, as so many grotesque facsimiles of the states of White peoples, and opposing them only on these terms. So everything converges towards a general levelling, and only the ugliest relationships of power and spheres of influence can be the determining factor of their development, even more so than in the past.

[NOTE: Until just the other day it was possible to see an interesting exception in Japan: the coexistence of a traditional culture and external modernisation. After the Second World War, however, this equilibrium has been increasingly altered to the advantage of modernisation, and the last bulwarks against it are falling, one after the other.]

Returning to our chief subject, we need to consider the third and most important factor of the Fascist turn to 'racism'. Here we can absolutely talk about continuity and coherence in respect to ideas always professed by Mussolini. There was a problem that interested Mussolini, and to which he believed that an important contribution could be made by racism in the proper, positive sense (that is, distinct from

---

194 Some spoke of a 'second wave of colonialism' during the Cold War, as both the United States and the Soviet Union were active in influencing politics, sometimes through direct intervention, in countries throughout the world, and most especially the Third World, in an effort to influence them to support their foreign policies aimed at countering the opposite power.

both anti-Semitism and from the defence of the prestige of the people/race—the 'Italian race'—before coloured peoples). This was the problem of the formation of a new type of Italian, to be differentiated in the rather fragile and anarchic temperamental substance of our people. (A substance presenting such characteristics was also far from corresponding to a certain homogeneous 'race'.) Mussolini thought—and he was not mistaken—that the future of Fascism and the nation depended not so much on the transmission of ideas and institutions as much as on a formative action that causes a selected 'type' to arise. Creating 'a new way of life' and 'a new type of Italian' had been a need felt by Mussolini from the very beginnings of the regime—and we saw that during a period in which there can certainly be no talk of Nazi influence, because Hitler had not yet attained power in 1929. In the report on the Vatican accords delivered in Parliament, Mussolini spoke of an action of the state that, in 'continually transforming the nation', could reach all the way to 'its physical aspect'. This is an idea that was closely connected to the general doctrine, which we have already discussed, of the relationship between state and people, as between 'form' and 'matter'.

This is exactly the positive and creative aspect of the issue of political racism. In principle we are not dealing with anything imaginary. History presents us with quite a few examples of races, not as given primal groups, but as groups that are formed with sufficiently stable characteristics in relation to a given culture and tradition, defined especially by a mode of being, by an 'interior race'. We can start out with the people of Israel, that originally was not a single pure and homogeneous race, but was instead an ethnic compound united and formed by a religious tradition, and which continued all the way to the United States, where an easily recognisable type was rapidly born from a rather unlikely ethnic mix because of the climate of a given culture, or rather pseudo-culture (this situation allows us to glimpse much greater possibilities when this process instead involves a real culture with a traditional character).

Moreover, we can aim at the ideal of human completeness. While the reference to race and blood could count as an objection against all that is individualism, intellectualism and superficial comportment, already from current expressions, such as 'thoroughbred', or *être racé*, which can be applied not only to a human being, but also to an animal, it was possible to reach a specific and unexceptional meaning of 'race'. It was a question of a true, maximal correspondence with the 'type' of each species, something that cannot be observed in the masses, but only in a restricted number of cases. All the protests of intellectuals, or of those who regard themselves as being 'spiritual', count for nothing against the consideration that it would only be good and beneficial if true values were defended by men that, even as physical race (*soma*)[195] and as character (race of soul) reproduce a higher type, instead of showing a painful break between body and spirit. In this regard, we can leave aside all modern 'racism' and refer to an ideal that is Classical, even Hellenic. This would mean that certain, almost hysterical, reactions to which some intellectuals and men of culture give way as soon as they hear talk of race, run the risk of being indicative only of the fact that they have not come to terms with 'race'.

We mentioned that 'The Manifesto of Race', which was compiled in 1938 as a prelude to the turn to racism by a small group of elements of a rather heterogeneous orientation,[196] raked up from here and there, was bungled and inconsistent, partly because of the complete lack of adequate preliminary studies in Italy. *Inter alia* the 'Manifesto' affirmed that the concept of race 'is a purely biological concept' and, apart from the use of the absurd term 'Italian race', asserted that 'the population of Italy today is of Aryan origin, and its civilisation is Aryan',[197] neglecting to indicate exactly what 'Aryan' was supposed to mean. In fact, this Aryan character was reduced to something negative and problematic, and consisted of not being Hebrew or from a coloured race, with no positive counterpart, nor any specification of a higher criterion to establish the comportment, style, worldview, or predispositions of character and spirit of the person who was to be called Aryan. The foreign influence here is clear, since it is specified that Fascist racism should be of 'Nordic-Aryan orientation'.

In the development of a serious ideology concerning race, all this would have had to be reconsidered and corrected. It happens to be the case that we can personally attest to the fact that Mussolini was absolutely inclined toward developments of this kind. Even before Fascism's

---

195 Classical Greek: 'body'.

196 There was a great deal of debate amongst those who contributed to the manifesto, many of whom had very different motivations and philosophical attitudes. The manifesto underwent so many revisions that some of those who worked on it demanded that their names be removed from the final version.

197 'The Manifesto of Race', p. 173.

racist turn, we had the opportunity to take a stance against racism[198] that was of a biological and scientific character, on the one hand, and collectivising and fanatical, on the other, such as prevailed in Germany, opposing to it a 'racism' that, while maintaining a vision of the ideal we have discussed of human completeness and interest, particularly emphasised what we called the 'inner race', asserting on this topic a traditional, anti-materialist conception of the human being. Moreover, the 'inner race' could have been the base and fulcrum for the formative action we have talked about. Even if it were right to propose a 'type' as the ideal and centre of crystallisation, it was not appropriate for Italy to refer to the Nordic-Aryan type, following the Germans. The science of origins had ascertained that different groups differentiated from a common primal stock ('Indo-European', 'Aryan'): on one side the Hellenic element (especially the Doric of Sparta), on another the basal Roman element, and finally the German element. Various typical traits of character, ethics, customs, worldview and culture shared by these three stocks attest this single, remote origin. Thus for this centre of crystallisation we could choose the 'Aryo-Roman' type with its characteristic gifts, which could constitute an adequate integration of Fascism's bold 'Roman' vocation on a concrete level, while remaining completely independent of German racism. We expounded these ideas, along with many others, in a book, *Synthesis of a Doctrine of Race*.[199] Mussolini read the book and invited me to meet him. It is symptomatic that he approved of its theses unconditionally, and finally agreed that we would undertake some rather significant initiatives based on the book. The crisis of events and certain internal doubts kept us from completing them.

Concretely it was a question of observing that a nation is not a 'race', and in every member of an historic nation there exist various components or possibilities. An adequate climate of high stress can create a situation where some of these possibilities get the upper hand and achieve a differentiation that can gradually reach the level of *soma*. As a particular case, some people have noted the delineation of a common physical type among members of particular bodies of men who have been assigned specific, demanding tasks (today, for instance, paratroopers and similar soldiers). A similar order of ideas obviously has nothing in common with

---

198 Evola began elaborating his doctrine of race in his essay 'Race and Culture' from 1934. He also wrote a book, *The Blood Myth*, in 1937 about race.

199 Julius Evola, *Sintesi di dottrina della razza*.

a lower racism or with vulgar anti-Semitism, and we believe that it can play a role in the context of values which are compatible with the action of a state of a hierarchical and traditional character.

[NOTE: We recalled above that anti-Semitism has existed in all times. In the Christian era it had a religious character, but it would be difficult to explain the constant aversion the same peoples nourished for the Hebrew based only upon the religious factor, without also introducing the factor of character. Modern anti-Semitism, on the other hand, has had a social basis. It can be traced back to the reaction provoked by the fact that Jews, who stick together in tight solidarity, have succeeded in ensuring themselves a pre-eminent position in the intellectual, economic and professional fields in various countries according to ratios that have no relationship to the actual proportion of the Jewish group in relation to the whole 'Aryan' population of the nations concerned (see *Notes on the Third Reich*, Chapter IV). If we want to be impartial, however, it is not fair to assert the simplistic social situation with which the appeal to 'race' could be reduced to a pretext for 'Get up! I want to sit there.' We would first need to define what it means to be Jewish (Judaism as an inner or spiritual race) and, aside from their numerical proportions in key positions, demonstrate that in individual cases, this way of being gives a special, undesirable direction to the relevant activity, perhaps even without the person in question being aware of it. Naturally 'race', in this sense — Judaism — has nothing to do with religion. Conversion to Christianity changes it as little as a similar conversion could change the constitution, heredity and innate dispositions of a Negro. This consideration explains the importance of the concept of inner race, that is, to prevent every one-sidedness. With reference to this, however, we have had the opportunity to state that today, anti-Jewish polemic makes little sense, given that the qualities that can be, perhaps, deprecated in Jews are found in the so-called 'Aryans' to no less a degree, without having the excuse of hereditary precedents. Speaking of American capitalism and considering the traditional relationship of Jews with trade, money and interest, Werner Sombart[200] could say, similarly, that to the degree that the Jew emancipated himself and rose in the modern epoch, to the same degree he transmitted his own mentality to the non-Hebrew.]

---

200 Evola is referring to his work, *The Jews and Modern Capitalism* (London: T. F. Unwin, 1913).

While we acknowledge the factors we mentioned and their related situations, and in particular remembering the arbitrary nature of a one-sided identification of racism with anti-Semitic fanaticism, we should not therefore consider the racist (if we insist on using this term) aspect of Fascism as an aberration, as imitation, or as a 'foreign body'.

In this context we could also make a general retrospective consideration concerning the entire Fascist experience. The intrinsic value of an idea and a system should be judged in itself, without all that enters into the world of contingency. The decisive factor, however, practically and historically, is the quality of the men who make themselves the affirmers and defenders of this idea and this system. If this quality is inferior, the intrinsic value of the principles will be of little help—and *vice versa*. It can happen that a system that is defective and has serious theoretical faults can function in a satisfying manner, at least for a certain period, when run by a qualified group and qualified leaders. This is the importance possessed by these values of 'race', in the generalised sense of spirit and character, and not the purely biological sense. We have spoken of this issue a while ago.

Granted this, we need to ask ourselves up to what point the negative side presented by Fascism, or which existed behind Fascism's ideological façade and revealed itself at the moment when Fascism was tested, should be referred, essentially, to the human factor. We shall not be afraid to turn the thesis of a certain anti-Fascism on its head in order to affirm that it was not Fascism that negatively affected the Italian people, the 'Italian race', but *vice versa*. It was this people, this 'race' that negatively affected Fascism, that is, the Fascist experiment, insofar as Italy could not furnish a sufficient number of men who could rise to the challenge of certain high demands and symbols, men who were healthy elements and able to promote the development of the positive potential that could have been contained in the Fascist system. This deficiency must also be taken into consideration in regard to really free men who could have worked, not outside Fascism or against it, but inside it. There was a lack of men who were capable of saying clearly and fearlessly to Mussolini what needed to be said, to make him understand what it was important that he understand, instead of indulging him in wishful thinking in accordance with his desires. (A notable case is what Mussolini was led to believe about the effective industrial and military potential of Italy to enter the war.) Of course, there were some men like this during the Twenty Years, but not enough of them. He should have asserted the ancient Roman maxim that a true leader does not want to be the boss of slaves, but to have at his side free men who follow him — to correct the mental dispositions that almost fatally tend to prevail, through human weakness, in anyone who holds power, and which encourage sycophancy. More generally, what must we think of the foundations on which Fascism rested in part, of the human material it had at its disposal, when we see the ease with which the hysterical popular masses disappeared like snow in the Sun, when the wind changed direction, and when we consider the number of ex-Fascists today who, accordingly, do not hesitate to declare that in the preceding period they were in bad faith, were acting out of mere conformism or opportunism, or had been brainwashed? The charge, in our opinion, should be brought in large measure against the 'Italian race'. We must come to the conclusion, which gives us little comfort, of their refractory character in regard to everything that can be regarded as alien to its 'tradition', making Fascism appear as a dark parenthesis, and the return to 'democracy' with all the rest (due only to the enemy's victory) as a 'second *Risorgimento*', with the complete separation from everything that can enter into the circle of the political and governmental ideals of a true Right.

As the reader has seen, throughout our critical discrimination in the area of doctrine, we have essentially referred to the Fascism of the Twenty Years. From the second Fascism, the Fascism of the Salò Republic, we believe that very little can be gathered in this regard, since too many contingent factors influenced what it presented as a first draft of state, political and social doctrine, and what was presented suffered from a complete lack of a period of calm maturation. Its value is to be found in its combatant and legionary aspect. As someone correctly observed, its value stands in the fact that, perhaps for the first time in all Italian history, the second Fascism saw a significant mass of Italians consciously choose the path of fighting in lost positions, of sacrifice and unpopularity in order to obey the principle of fidelity to a leader and military honour. In this sense, it rose from what resisted a test of fire. Beyond any ideology and party spirit — we want to emphasise this point — from the purely moral and existential point of view, we can say that it is with the second Fascism that the 'Italian race' in this crisis gave a positive account of itself by associating itself with everything that the simple Italian soldier, in a regular military division or in the battalions of the Blackshirt, could give on the battlefields.

[NOTE: On 28 September 1943, the journal Politica Nuova published an article with the title 'Considerations Concerning the Facts about Italy', which Mussolini caused to be republished as a pamphlet for mass distribution, indicating that he shared the ideas expressed in it. The article was a kind of self-criticism of certain aspects of Fascism and the weaknesses that existed inside it. Some accusations deserve to be reproduced here. The article accused the political class of the regime 'of having formed an increasingly thick barrier between Mussolini and the Fascist masses so that the Duce could not notice other possible collaborators. Therefore every Fascist of any worth was considered positively dangerous if he had contacts with the Duce, and was literally persecuted until he was convinced to return to obscurity or, if he resisted, until he was politically pulverised'. The second accusation is 'of having adopted the method of changing the guard in rotation, in a narrow and hermetic system of political complicity and material interests in the managerial sectors of the regime; of having abused Mussolini's trust to the extent of often hiding from him and falsifying to him the situation of the regime and the mood of the country even at the most critical hours, casting upon the shoulders of the Duce the responsibility, or even the initiative of provisions and directives that did not belong to him'. We should remember all this when we hear people claim, "The lesson of Italian Fascism shows us the dangers and limitations of a man isolated by his own power' or 'the insufficiency and danger of pure Caesarism which Fascism was reduced to at the end' (M. Bardèche).[201] We must not neglect the part that the Italian human substance played in good measure here, which we have indicated, with attitudes that were quite different from those that were required by the strict idea of an Order—the only corrective for this isolation.

Again, this article, concerning the war, made the accusation of 'having first compromised the conduct of the war, notwithstanding the abundant exercises of a shoddy rhetorical patriotism, and having then caused the military catastrophe through the natural avoidance of every supreme test that could not so much compromise the fate of the nation,

201 Maurice Bardèche (1907-1998) was a French writer who supported fascism internationally during the 1930s, but refused to support the Vichy government of France under German occupation. Robert Brasillach, one of the most prominent French intellectuals who supported Vichy, was his brother-in-law. Throughout the remainder of his life, he sought a resurrection of the fascist ideal in Europe.

but disturb the fate of the lifestyles of its people, which was until then prosperous and tranquil'.

To have an acknowledgment of all this, even when it was too late, is noteworthy.]

XII

Some final considerations should be dedicated to the Fascist idea insofar as it was a factor in the alliances and constellations of world political forces.

In the first place, it is possible to indicate the possible counterpart to the developments in Italian foreign policy that led to Italy's rapprochement with Germany, the Rome-Berlin Axis, and finally to the so-called 'Tripartite Pact'[202] at the start of the Second World War.

Even in this regard, the judgment of various people who are not anti-Fascist in principle suffers from a kind of complex. We should not, however, hide the fact that in Italy, aside from high-level diplomatic activities, the rapprochement with Germany was not very popular. An earlier ideology that ended by influencing the feelings of various strata of the nation played a role in this. From a certain 'patriotic history' of Masonic-liberal confection and inspired by the *Risorgimento*, the German (accompanied, moreover, by the Austrian) has been depicted as a sort of age-old enemy of the Italian people. (The mystifications of this history reached the point of absurdly attributing a 'national' significance to the revolt of the communes against the Holy Roman Empire[203] and its representative, Friedrich II.)[204] Aside from that, however, we need to think about everything that derived from the inability of the Italian 'matter' to endure the 'form' that Fascism wanted to impress upon it.

We have mentioned the real affinities that existed in orientation and typical virtues between Sparta, ancient Rome and the German stocks. On the other hand, there is a clear difference between the Roman and

---

202 The Tripartite Pact was a military alliance between Germany, Italy and Japan that was signed on 27 September 1940.

203 The communes were city-states which retained a degree of independence from their rulers in the Holy Roman Empire. In the 1240s, some of the Italian communes sided with the Guelphs in the opposition of Pope Innocent IV to the Emperor, with great success.

204 Frederick II (1194-1250) was Emperor of the Holy Roman Empire, and he was supported by the Ghibellines.

the 'Latin' and, in part, the Italian as a temperament, style and world-view. To the degree to which Fascism returned to the Roman symbol, trying to ensure a reformation of its politics and ethics, it was natural that it would attempt a revision both of the 'Latin' myth and of the anti-German one. About the first, Mussolini could speak of 'bastard brotherhoods'. In regard to the second, in the qualities of discipline, order, military capacity, love for authority and seriousness presented by the peoples of Central Europe, especially with reference to the Prussian ideal, he had to notice that these were closer to what belonged also to the ancient Roman character in its best or primitive period, while they were far from those that had come to prevail in the substance of the Latin peoples, and therefore also of the Italian people, in its individualist, undisciplined, careless and petit bourgeois aspects, given the penchant of Italy for tourists, mandolins, gondoliers, museums, ruins, 'O Sole Mio', and so on, despite a background of humble, hardworking folk who are loyal to their old customs. [NOTE: On this, see our book *Men Among the Ruins*, Chapter XIV.]

Thus, from the point of view of ideals, we can perfectly well speak of intrinsic affinities. Making Italy 'Roman' and Fascist (wherever we can give a positive sense to the second term—and in this regard, we ought to remember all the reservations formulated in the course of the present essay) could be the same as, to a certain degree, giving it a Prussian stamp. As for political orientation, Italian history could offer a precedent in the Ghibelline[205] movement, which had Dante among its advocates, and who were the exponents of a large part of the Italian nobles of the epoch. It is flabbergasting that during the period of the Axis, Fascism never made use of the Ghibelline myth, perhaps because of the intellectual background and social origins of Mussolini and all those who were close to him.

It follows from these considerations that the diplomatic dealings with Germany that led to the Rome-Berlin Axis could have met a positive response with a less contingent, deeper and more vocational character on the level of ideals. [NOTE: For the Tripartite Pact we could point

---

205 Ghibelline is a thirteenth century term which was originally coined to name the supporters of the imperial power of the Hohenstaufen throne against Papal authority. They were in conflict with the Guelphs, who favoured the rule of the Pope. Evola saw this conflict as highlighting the distinction between priestly and royal authority in the state, since he believed the Ghibelline view to be the only valid one from a traditional perspective. He discusses this at length in *Revolt Against the Modern World* and *The Mystery of the Grail*.

out another basis for elective affinities,[206] since in Japan (at that time) the nation was held to be founded on an Emperor who ruled by divine right, as well as on the samurai (the warrior nobility) and their ethic. But obviously in this regard, there was no direct relation granted the great diversities of race, history and environment.] At the same time, however, the response to the Axis reveals the inmost feelings found in part of the 'Italian race', and even various exponents of Fascism (a typical case: Galeazzo Ciano):[207] the intolerance of, resistance to and lack of sympathy for the rapprochement with Germany. We do not wish, however, to insist on seeing only one side of the issue. Thus, to explain the rapprochement there are other factors to take into consideration, such as the two nations' concrete common interests, the personal sympathy between the two 'dictators', and the affinities between the two movements, Fascism and National Socialism, on the basis of their populist aspects, on which we have already expressed our judgment. Nonetheless, the fact remains that Mussolini was particularly impressed by the fact that in Hitler's Germany, there was a clear continuation of the German and Prussian ethic, tradition and conception of the state.

On the other hand, a direct consequence of the nature of the doctrine and worldview affirmed by Fascism was a natural opposition to both the world of the Western democracies and capitalism (the extreme expression of which is embodied by the United States) and the world of Communism and Soviet Russia—to use contemporary terminology, both 'West' and 'East'. Therefore, the military alignment of Italy in the Second World War proceeded in principle from the logic of Fascist ideology and the values it affirmed. In theory, there is nothing to object to in this.

Considerations of a different sort that could be made about the war would take us away from our theme. We have already indicated that it

---

206 'Elective affinities' was originally a scientific term, referring to the fact that chemicals display a preference to combine with certain other chemicals, and not with others. Goethe later adopted this term to refer to the same phenomenon in human relationships, explaining why individuals prefer to relate with certain people rather than others. Goethe's third novel, which uses the term as its title, explores this phenomenon, and this is also the way in which Evola uses it.

207 Galeazzo Ciano (1903-1944) was the Minister of Foreign Affairs, and was Mussolini's son-in-law. He opposed Italy's involvement in the Second World War, and voted in favor of Mussolini's dismissal from office in 1943. After being dismissed from his post by the Badoglio government, Ciano attempted to resettle in Germany, but the Germans turned him over to the Italian Social Republic, where he was executed for treason.

would be illegitimate to draw any conclusion from the war's outcome about the intrinsic value of the ideology that led Italy to participate in it alongside Germany and under the banner of the Tripartite Pact. The problem to pose, not only for Italy, but also and especially for Germany, would be that of the degree to which the war was conducted with precise knowledge of the possibilities and a sense of limits. Of course, hindsight has 20/20 vision. It cannot be denied that after the collapse of the Western front of the Allies, and with only England still resisting in the midst of a desperate situation and awaiting an invasion, only a minority could doubt that the game was about to end with a decisive victory for Germany and foresee that Italy, through her intervention, would instead become involved in events that Mussolini could not have the power to control and check in any way.

(We should not forget that Mussolini had done his best to prevent the outbreak of the Second World War at the last moment with an initiative that found no good will, especially from France. We should not forget, in addition, that Mussolini had earlier proposed the formation of the 'Quadripartite Pact'[208]—an understanding involving Germany, England, Italy and France—a formula that could have had a fundamental European importance, but which clashed with the ideological biases and the narrow horizons of the proposed partners.)

Moreover, we believe that even if, as we have said, by and large and in the abstract, the fronts of the Second World War appeared ideologically logical, it is also necessary to attribute the dire consequences to a lack of a sense of limits, a fanaticism, and finally an effective megalomania on Hitler's part. In reality, the first cause that led to the conflicts was Hitler's obsession with the myth of the people/race according to the formula of its unity with a single *Reich* and a single *Führer* ('*Ein Volk, ein Reich, ein Führer*').[209] If Germany had limited itself to rising again from the condition to which its defeat in the First World War had brought it and to becoming a great European power again; if, in its rise and expansion, it had had a sense of limit; if it could have stopped, without losing sight of its inevitable adversaries, and waited for conditions that might have been more propitious for acting in isolation against those forces that Hitler instead brought down upon himself all at the

---

208 The Quadripartite Pact was actually signed by all four nations on 7 June 1933, but the French Parliament refused to ratify it.

209 German: 'one people, one empire, one leader', a popular slogan of the Third Reich.

same time, dragging Italy with him—the state of Europe today would be very different.

Naturally, that state would be deprecated by different elements that were present in Germany, but even more so in Italy, that warmly hoped for the military defeat of their nation, indeed the nation's ruin, because it would entail the fall of the incumbent governments. [NOTE: Among them was Benedetto Croce.[210] An opponent of Italy's intervention against Germany in the First World War (he said then that one could only bring 'weak rationalisations' against Germany') and an admirer of Hegel, the philosopher of the authoritarian Prussian state, until 1925 a defender of the strong state in Italy, did not hesitate to state publically in the post-war period that he had desired the enemy's victory in the Second World War, and had favoured it 'with thought, sentiment and action', because he had understood that the Allies were not conducting 'a simple war of political and economic interests, but a war of religion' [sic]—as General Eisenhower did not hesitate to call the war in Europe a 'crusade'. There is only the small problem that the atheist Soviet Union figured among the Allies, and indeed played a decisive part in the outcome of the war, a nation committed to combat every religion as the 'opium of the people' and as a 'counterrevolutionary' factor. After Italy's collapse, like various anti-Fascists, Croce expressed bitter repentances, which have naturally been greeted with silence by those who today exalt Croce the anti-Fascist.] And unfortunately, in the events of the Italian war, there is no lack of cases in which it is difficult to say, to this very day, to what extent the lack of preparation and incompetence of certain high commands was connected with sabotage, if not downright treason.

For those who are not in principle anti-Fascist, things should appear in a rather different light. Above all, we should not exclude the possibility of corrective developments that, once the war was won, could have taken place in the two regimes to the extent of causing their positive aspects to prevail. Especially, there could have been the contribution of the fighting spirit of the veterans. As the veterans of the First World War reacted against the political and social climate they found on their return to their home country and so gave rise to a renovating movement, it would be equally probable that elements tempered in the new war would, upon their return, have caused a renovation of the regimes'

---

210 Benedetto Croce (1866-1952) was a highly influential Italian art critic, senator, and a philosopher in the German Idealist tradition. He initially supported Italian Fascism, but by 1925 he had become an opponent of the regime.

cadres, accompanied by the elimination of various negative aspects of the system and various individual traits while the basic ideas remained.

There is the well-known propaganda which has been organised in unprecedented proportions that, especially concerning Germany, presents everything that happened in the period before and during the war as a unique ensemble of evil ideas, degraded policies and horrors, with special attention given to the German Gestapo and the Italian OVRA (Organization for Vigilance and the Repression of Anti-Fascism),[211] the concentration camps and so on, with all the exaggerations, illegitimate generalisations, and sometimes downright inventions that are useful for that purpose. We have no intention of asserting that everything was in order then, and various things deserve to be severely condemned and deprecated. But every revolution or war has had its dark side, and there is no reason why those things should be held against the Third Reich alone that are willingly passed over in silence by the interested parties in regard to, let us say, the European wars of religion, the French Revolution, or the Bolshevik Revolution that led to the Soviet regime. The method of ascribing to one's adversaries every horror and crime, while hiding or denying one's own, is well-known, but has never been so systematically and impudently applied as during and after the Second World War. Remembering all that we have said about possible later corrections and normalisations of the system, we can say that no price would have been too high, supposing the war had proven victorious by some miracle (given the enormous disproportion of the material forces that decided it) and had the following results: breaking the backbone of Soviet Russia and very likely provoking the crisis of Communism itself (instead of the Communist takeover of all the European countries on the other side of the 'Iron Curtain' and the current Cold War between 'East' and 'West' that, for good or ill, is still going on); humiliating the United States and expelling it from European politics (instead of a Western Europe that, in its own defence, is more or less at the mercy of the United States and its presidents); crippling British power but certainly, despite the probability that some of its colonies would have fallen into other hands, to a much lesser degree than happened to 'victorious' England, which has seen its empire broken up (exactly the same thing that happened to 'victorious' France); preventing, when it was still possible, the Communist takeover of China as a result of the victory of Japan, instead of the rise

---

211 The Italian secret police, an organisation which was created in 1927.

of a new, powerful and very dangerous home in Asia for worldwide sub-version; impeding the insurrection of coloured peoples and the end of European hegemony, because never—and again never—in the 'New Order', under the banner of the ideas defended by the peoples of the Axis, would there have been a place for the self-destructive psychosis of anti-colonialism, nor could that revolt have counted on help from the Soviet Union. All people with sentiments that are not necessarily 'Fascist', but who are of the Right, when they allow their imagination to dwell on such possibilities and overcome their current prejudices, have no choice but to draw up a balance sheet and adequately measure the distance that separates them from what instead presents itself to our eyes as the current world situation.

XIII

After these few considerations, we can end our examination, which, although brief, can perhaps furnish the basis for a critical judgment on the structures and meaning of Fascism from a point of view that is different from either a confused and one-sided exaltation or an *a priori* denigration. The essential task is to introduce criteria that may lead beyond the rather restricted horizon found in one or the other of these two points of view.

On this topic, it is relevant to discuss the unusual character of the 'exceptional' laws that have been promulgated in Italy against Fascism and the defence of Fascism and that are still in force, although admittedly in a somewhat revised form.

We can admit that a 'democracy' may defend itself with legislative measures, if we are referring to a procedural political form, but not to a dogmatic and univocal doctrinal system, because in this second case the 'definitions' of democracy are multiple and discordant and because, above all, we would find ourselves before a singular contradiction. However paradoxical it could seem, democratic 'freedom of opinion' should entail the admission of the legitimacy of professing and defending even anti-democratic ideas, if it is not to create a regime of bullying and tyranny, although with the flag turned upside down. (Anyhow, more than one writer has noted that few regimes are as intolerant and fanatic as the ones that proclaim 'liberty'.)

What democracy as method can have the right to combat would be only a praxis intended to conquer power and gain control of the state by violent means and direct action. To the degree that the legislation we mentioned aimed only at this by prosecuting the reconstruction of the Fascist Party as a crime, there would be nothing to object to. (We should not forget, however, that in Italy, Fascism ultimately came to power by an invitation to form a government made by the sovereign, and in Germany, Nazism paved its way by a parliamentary and plebiscitary majority.)

When, however, the legislation we are talking about has proposed not only to suppress certain outer manifestations (the Fascist salute, black shirts, Fascist hymns, etc.), but also to punish the 'defence of Fascism' as a crime, we have the juridical absurdity of fixing the punishment without first rigorously defining the terms of the crime—in our case: defining rigorously, above all, what we must understand by 'Fascism' and 'Fascist'. But this absurdity derives from a factual impossibility. In fact, it will appear very clear to those who have followed us up to this point that those who would like to condemn or attack Fascism as a whole would find themselves compelled also to condemn ideas and principles that did not belong only to Fascism, but were important in other, earlier systems as well. In these terms, it would be necessary to define as more or less 'Fascist' the greater part of the states that history describes from distant ages, when they are based on a principle of authority and hierarchy and admit nothing similar to absolute democracy, liberalism or socialism.

To be intellectually coherent and to avoid demonstrating an open bias, serious legislation for a democracy's self-defence would have to proceed in another way: it would have to begin from a definition of a general system that is constitutionally unacceptable, of which 'Fascism' (obviously Fascism in certain of its aspects) is only a particular case, a system that, if you prefer, could also be called 'totalitarian' in the worse sense, as we have already explained. The definition ought to have a rigorously structural and objective character, without labels. But everyone can see that the first victim of serious legislation imposed on such a basis would have to be Communism, and the law would lead to the immediate dissolution and banning of the Communist Party in a democratic state. This is exactly what the United States did,[212] and earlier on the Federal Republic of Germany in Bonn,[213] with greater coherence than we have shown.

The fact is, however, that legislation was passed against Fascism in Italy without introducing as its precise counterpart an even stricter legislation against Communism and Communist propaganda. (Everyone knows everything that can be charged to the Communist Party, as an activist organisation which trains its forces, possesses deposits of arms

---

212 The United States never actually banned Communism, but Evola is probably referring to the efforts of the House Committee on Un-American Activities to stem Communism, beginning in 1947.

213 The West German government banned the Communist Party of Germany in 1956, although it was reconstituted in 1968 under a different name.

and networks of 'cells', receives foreign financing, and so on. These activities call for measures very different from those enacted against the much-feared 'reconstruction of the Fascist Party'.) This fact shows that we are facing an orientation determined not by a rigorous juridical thought, but by a partisan spirit, and a democracy that is in reality subject to the forces of the Left and Communism, which, as is known, ranks among its tactics using democracy so as to later bury the same democracy, by taking advantage of the foolishness, infatuation and cowardice of democracy's representatives.

If this partisan spirit, this foolishness and infatuation in contemporary Italy had not reached the limit of real irresponsibility, it would be natural to acknowledge the importance of the rise and organisation of a national movement as an antidote to a sickness that is now widespread and lurking in all the structures of the country. Two eminent sociologists, Pareto and Mosca,[214] have correctly emphasised that after the rise of an industrialised mass society, with a large-scale development of public services, the modern state finds itself dangerously paralysed in the means by which it previously defended its authority. In an emergency situation, the trade union organisations and, in general, that of the mass of workers, would only need to issue an appeal for strikes and sabotage to block the entire national organism. The police force and even the army would not be able to respond effectively. Given the point the Communist cancer has now reached in Italy, it would seem clearly advisable to establish a national movement that could gradually create a pervasive network intended to rapidly furnish elements to confront this group everywhere—in factories, public services, offices, and so on—in emergency cases. Its purpose would be especially, and first of all, defending the state and the state's authority (even when it is an 'empty state') against disruptive public demonstrations, not the negation of both state and authority. The importance that a movement of the Right would have in these terms seems, however, to escape the present managers of democratic Italy—a political class far worse than all its predecessors—who acknowledge only the psychosis of 'Fascism' and can only come up with 'extraordinary laws' of which we have already indicated all their superficiality and one-sidedness.

* * *

214 Gaetano Mosca (1858-1941) was an Italian political scientist who particularly studied the role of elites in societies.

We said at the beginning that, if we could not be asked to expound here a complete political doctrine of the Right, even this critical examination might furnish, step by step, some reference points. We believe that this has been done. The result, however, will perhaps be disconcerting for many readers. It will be necessary, in fact, to measure the distance between an intransigent political doctrine of the Right and everything that exists today on the level of both political reality and ideology. Aside from the national movement we just discussed, which would have value especially as a work force for an almost physical defence, we need to ask ourselves what groups or men today would have the courage to take up and defend these positive elements that we have isolated in Fascism without compromise, while also clearly emphasising the monarchical, aristocratic and hierarchical idea, or that which we have elaborated by separating out the negative and sufficiently integrating the positive tasks that needed to be faced under Fascism.

As things stand today, there is good reason to think that a critical examination like the one attempted in the preceding pages has a purely theoretical significance. It can be of interest only because, as far as we know, no one, not only in Italy but also in all of Europe, has undertaken a study of this kind before now, which is separated from partisan passions and from everything that reflects the world of contingency and which adheres to often forgotten ideas of a higher tradition. For what concerns not a simple testimony, but also a practical decision, perhaps things could appear otherwise only in the desirable eventuality that things reach a real crisis, instead of a definitive collapse achieved by those means that democratic legality puts at the disposal of the forces of worldwide subversion. In such a crisis, by a reaction of the national organism analogous to the reactions that sometimes occur unexpectedly in an individual physical organism when its vital forces are threatened, the only alternatives that could materialise would be the ones predicted by Donoso Cortès and mentioned by us, the choice between 'absolute negations' and 'sovereign affirmations'. Nothing, however, allows us to pronounce on all this today, when every single practical goal is foreign to the motivation behind the present essay.

As the conclusion of the present essay we can indicate, in summary, what are the most essential traits of the type of state and regime that could be defined starting from a movement with a 'Fascist' character, which would overcome the various oscillations and confusions present in earlier reconstructive currents in a direction that is decisively of the

Right. As a reference point we should, however, consider not what Italian Fascism and similar movements were in their factual reality, that is, in their simple, unrepeatable 'historicity'. What in 'Fascism' survives, and which retains its value and relevance, are its potentialities—as someone correctly said, it is what 'it could have and ought to have been', if certain conditions had been realised.

The clear stance against every form of democracy and socialism is the first characteristic of the state of which we spoke. It will put an end to the stupid infatuation, cowardice and hypocrisy of those who today chatter of 'democracy', who proclaim democracy, who exalt democracy. Democracy is only a regressive, crepuscular phenomenon.

The true state will then be oriented against both capitalism and Communism. At its centre will stand a principle of authority and a transcendent symbol of sovereignty. The most natural incarnation of such a symbol is the monarchy. The need to confer a chrism on this transcendence is of fundamental importance.

Monarchy is not incompatible with a 'legal dictatorship', more or less as it was in ancient Roman law.[215] The sovereign can confer exceptional unitary powers on a person of special stature and qualification, still on a legal basis, when there are special situations to overcome or exceptional tasks to confront.

We can accept the formula of 'authoritarian constitutionalism'. It entails overcoming the fetish and mythology of the so-called 'rule of law'. Law is not born from anything perfectly formed, nor with characteristics of eternal, immutable validity. At the origin of every law stands a relationship of force. This power that is at the origin of every law can intervene, suspending and modifying the current structures when the situation demands it, attesting with this action that there still exists in the political organism a will and a sovereignty, that it is not reduced to something abstract, mechanical and soulless.

The state is the primary element that precedes nation, people and 'society'. The state—and with the state everything that is properly constituted as political order and political reality—is defined essentially on the basis of an idea, not by naturalistic and contractual factors.

---

215 In ancient Rome, the Senate had the ability to appoint a dictator in an emergency situation involving a war within the state itself. This dictator was invested with absolute political and military power, including over the Senate itself. The position only continued until the crisis had passed.

Not a social contract,[216] but relations of loyalty and obedience, of free subordination and honour, are the bases of the true state, which does not acknowledge demagoguery and populism.

The true state is organic and unified without being 'totalitarian'. The relations we are discussing allow for the possibility of a large margin of decentralisation. Liberty and partial autonomy stand in relation to loyalty and responsibility according to a precise reciprocity. When these relations are broken, the power that is concentrated at the centre, manifesting its own nature, will therefore intervene with a severity and harshness in proportion to the liberty that was conceded.

The true state does not acknowledge the system of parliamentary democracy and party rule (*partitocrazia*). It can admit only corporative representations that are differentiated and articulated through a Lower or Corporative House. Above that will stand an Upper House as an extraordinary tribunal to guarantee the pre-eminence of the political principal, and having higher goals which are not only material and short-term.

It will be necessary to take a resolute stance against the aberrant system of indiscriminate universal suffrage and 'one man, one vote' which now includes the female sex. The formula of 'politicising the masses' should be rejected. The majority of a healthy and ordered nation should not be involved in politics. The Fascist trinity, 'authority, order and justice',[217] retains its unshaken validity for the true state.

The political party, which is a necessary organ for a movement in a period of transition and struggle, should not be replaced by a 'single party' once power is conquered and the system is stabilised. Its quite different task will be to establish something like an Order, which will participate in the dignity and authority concentrated in the centre, and assume some of the functions that in earlier, traditional regimes belonged to the nobility as a political class in key positions of the state (for example in the army and the diplomatic corps). The premise of this class was a stricter ethic and a special lifestyle. This nucleus will also act as the guardian of the idea of the state, and will prevent the 'caesarean' isolation of whoever exercises the supreme authority.

---

216 The idea of the social contract, which was instrumental in the development of modern democracy, is that individuals surrender some of their personal freedom to their political leaders, as well as to society as a whole, in return for the benefits and defense of their other liberties that are offered by living in the society.

217 A popular slogan of the Fascists.

The sphere of politics and power should be, by its very nature and function, free from economic influences, influences by economic groups or special interests. It is appropriate to recall the statement of Sulla,[218] who said that his ambition was not to possess gold, but to hold power over those who possess it.

The corporative reform should take place within the concrete world of labour and production, that is, in the businesses, through a new, organic structuring of them and a decisive elimination of class spirit, class struggle, and the different mentalities that call themselves 'capitalist', proletarian or Marxist. The trade union movement must be rejected. It is the greatest tool of all the subversive movements of recent times, and is the real cancer of the democratic state. As in the Fascist conception, it will be the state's task to act as referee, moderator and decider in the case of conflicts and disruptions. The objectivity and rigour of this higher court, which needs to be made concrete in adequate structures, will allow the abolition of the tool of the strike. The abuses of strikes, their use for blackmail and the other purposes for which they are used, which are more often political than social and economic, have become increasingly obvious and indefensible.

The defence of the principle of true justice will entail denouncing what is today continually promoted as 'social justice', a justice that serves only the lowest classes of society (the so-called 'working classes') and works to the detriment of other classes, effectively leading to injustice. The true state will also be hierarchical, especially because it will be able to acknowledge and create respect for the hierarchy of true values, giving primacy to values of a higher order, not material or utilitarian ones, and admitting relevant, legitimate inequalities or differences of social positions, opportunities and dignity. The true state will reject as aberrant the formula of the state of labour, whether or not this state is presented as 'national'.

The vital condition of every true state is a well-defined climate: the climate of the highest possible tension, but not of forced agitation. It will be desirable that everyone stay at his post, that he takes pleasure in an activity in conformity with his own nature and vocation, which is therefore free and desired for itself before considering utilitarian purposes

---

218 Lucius Cornelius Sulla (c. 138 -78 BCE) was a Roman general who served as consul of the Roman Republic twice, as well as dictator. He was particularly noted for having voluntarily given up the powers of dictator and restoring the constitutional government.

and the unhealthy desire to live above one's proper condition. If it is not possible to ask everyone to follow an 'ascetic and military vision of life', it will be possible to aim at a climate of concentrated intensity, of personal life, that will encourage people to prefer a greater margin of liberty, as opposed to comfort and prosperity paid for with the consequent limitation of liberty through the evitable economic and social influences. Autarchy, in the terms we have emphasised, is a valid Fascist formula. A course of virile, measured austerity is also valid and, finally, an internal discipline through which one develops a taste and an anti-bourgeois orientation of life, but no schoolmarmish and impertinent intrusion by what is public into the field of private life. Here, too, the principle should be liberty connected with equal responsibility and, in general, giving prominence to the principles of 'great morality' as opposed to the principles of conformist 'little morality'.

In essence, the climate of the true state should be personalising, animating and free. An inner force should produce a potential orbiting of individuals, groups, partial unities and men of an Order around a centre. This orbiting is one of which we should acknowledge the 'anagogic' and integrative character. It is integrative also in relation to the fact, which is not at all paradoxical, that true personality is realised only if it is affected by references to what is more than personal. Ultimately on this plane, through the rise and life of the true state, 'imponderables' come into play, as though predestined, because no oppressive and direct initiative can create and maintain this kind of climate.

In the context of a similar state, and under the sign of a relevant conception of life, a people can develop and achieve a calm, an internal force and a stability which does not mean stasis or stagnation, but rather the equilibrium of a concentrated power that, when the call is made, can cause everyone to rise immediately to their feet and makes them capable of absolute commitment and irresistible action.

A doctrine of the state can only propose values to test the elective affinities and the dominant or latent vocations of a nation. If a people cannot or does not want to acknowledge the values that we have called 'traditional', and which define a true Right, it deserves to be left to itself. At most, we can point out to it the illusions and suggestions of which it has been or is the victim, which are due to a general action which has often been systematically organised, and to regressive processes. If not even this leads to a sensible result, this people will suffer the fate that it has created, by making use of its 'liberty'.

Index

A

Alighieri, Dante 108
America, see United States of America
Anschluss 56, 73
Anti-Christ, Ecce Homo, Twilight of the Idols, The (Nietzsche) 63
anti-Semitism 93–94, 98, 102
Aristotle 16, 32
Aryan 94–95, 100–102
Austria 13, 20, 42–43, 56, 73
Austria-Hungary 20
Austrian Empire 20
Aventine secession (1924) 70
Axis 44, 55, 93, 107–109, 113

B

Bava-Beccaris massacre 20
Belgium 27
Bernanos, Georges 91
Beyond Good and Evil (Nietzsche) 63
Bismarck, Otto von 53–54
Blackshirts (Italy) 44, 60, 67
Blueshirts (Italy) 39
Bolshevik Revolution 112
Bonn 115
Bucharest 41

C

capitalism 9, 31, 79–80, 83–84, 86, 90–91, 102–103, 109, 118
Carlyle, Thomas 63
Catholicism 13–14, 33, 38

Central Powers (1914) 31
Chamber of Deputies 70, 72, 74–76
Chamber of Corporations 9, 75
Christian democracy 46
Ciano, Galeazzo 109
Codreanu, Corneliu 27, 41
Cold War 82, 98, 112
colonialism 96–98, 113
Communism 18, 29, 31, 41, 59, 63, 76, 86, 109, 112, 115–116, 118
Communist Party (Italy) 11, 22, 61, 115–116
Concordat (Vatican) 8, 13, 38
Congress of Vienna (1815) 53
'Considerations Concerning the Facts about Italy' 105
Corporatism 76–77, 79–80, 86
Corradini, Enrico 97
Crispi, Francesco 20
Croce, Benedetto 111

D

Dachau 42
Decline of the West, The (Spengler) 65
De Felice, Renzo 28
democracy 9, 13, 15, 18, 20–22, 31, 35, 39, 41, 43, 46, 57, 61–62, 67, 70–73, 76, 86, 90, 95, 104, 114–116, 118–119
di Rudinì, Antonio Starabba marchese 20

'Doctrine of Fascism, The'
  (Mussolini) 8, 29, 31, 32, 36, 45,
  92, 96
Donoso Cortès, Juan 28, 117

E

Eisenhower, Dwight 111
England 75, 96, 110, 112
Entente Cordiale 21
Ethiopia 10, 13, 53–54, 89, 96–97

F

Falange (Spain) 27, 67
Falangism 80
fasces 12, 44, 55, 74–75
Fascist Grand Council 54, 64, 74
Federal Republic of Germany (West
  Germany) 43–44, 81, 115
Ferrara 76
First World War 21, 30, 32, 41, 53,
  56, 95, 110–111
France 14, 19–21, 31, 53, 56, 70,
  94, 96, 105, 110, 112
Friedrich II 107
French Revolution (1789) 19, 23,
  28, 32, 56, 78, 112

G

Gay Science, The (Nietzsche) 36
Gentile, Giovanni 8, 29, 45, 76
German Labour Front 82
Germany 10, 20, 25, 28, 31–32,
  39–40, 42–44, 53–56, 62, 65,
  69, 81–82, 85, 87, 89, 94, 101,
  107–112, 115
Gestapo 112
Ghibellines 107
Guelphs 107–108
Guénon, René 6, 9, 14, 16, 39

H

Habsburgs 56
Heathen Imperialism (Evola) 14–15,
  33, 38
Hebrews (see also Jews) 94
Hegel, G. W. F. 25, 111
Heinrich, Walter 42
Hitler, Adolf 13, 15, 33, 55–56, 87,
  95, 99, 109–110
Hitler and the Vatican (Godman) 33
Hohenstaufens 108
Holy Roman Empire 107
Hungary 20, 73

I

Imperium 33, 44
Indo-European 101
Institute of Roman Studies 34
Interpretations of Fascism (De
  Felice) 28
Iron Curtain 112
Iron Guard 27, 41
Israel 94, 99
Italian Empire (1936) 53
Italian Foreign Policy 1870-1940
  (Lowe & Marzari) 68
Italian Nationalist Association 39, 97
Italian Republican Party 22
Italian Social Republic 10, 26, 45,
  51, 60, 83, 104, 109
Italian Socialist Party 70

J

Jews (see also Hebrews) 93–94,
  102–103
John Paul II, Pope 63

K

Keyserling, Hermann Graf von 39
Kingdom of Italy 13, 20, 38, 55–56,
  75

L

Länder 43
Lateran Treaty, see Concordat
    (Vatican)
Leibniz, Gottfried Wilhelm 79
liberalism 15, 18, 20, 31, 40, 67, 115
Lictors 44, 55
London Charter 69

M

Madrid 67
March on Rome 8, 26, 31, 51–52,
    60
Matteotti, Giacomo 70
Matthew, Book of 37
Marxism 18, 86, 89
Men Among the Ruins (Evola) 6, 8–9,
    13–14, 16, 23, 108
Metternich, Klemens von 53
Middle Ages 78
Milan 6–8, 10, 20, 61, 63, 87
Mill, John Stuart 18
Mosca, Gaetano 116
*Mussolini: As Revealed in His
    Political Speeches, 1914–1923*
    (Mussolini) 62
Mussolini, Benito 8–16, 24, 26,
    28–29, 31–33, 36, 38, 42, 44–45,
    51–56, 60–62, 64–66, 68, 70–71,
    76–78, 80, 83, 86–87, 89–90,
    93–99, 101, 104–105, 108–110
Mystery of the Grail, The (Evola) 108

N

National Socialism 2, 6, 25, 27, 29,
    41, 59, 80–81, 85–86, 94–95,
    109, 115
Negroes 97
Nemesis 56
Nazism, see National Socialism
Nietzsche, Friedrich 36, 63, 65

Nordic 101
North America 7
Notes on the Third Reich (Evola) 81,
    102
Nuremberg Trials 69

O

'On Liberty' (Mill) 18
On the Genealogy of Morals
    (Nietzsche) 63
'O Sole Mio' 108
Organization for Vigilance and the
    Repression of Anti-Fascism 112
Ottoman Empire 31

P

Pact of London (1915) 21
Pact of Steel 93
Palazzo Venezia 61
Pareto, Vilfredo 46, 116
Paul VI, Pope 14, 63
Perugia 61
Piedmont 9, 19–20, 52
Plato 47
Politica Nuova 105
Pope 14–15, 63, 107–108
Portugal 27, 80
Primo de Rivera, José Antonio 27,
    67
Prison Notes, The (Codreanu) 41
Prussia 67, 73

R

race 8, 10, 41, 93–97, 99–105,
    109–110, 128
racism 8, 10, 93–94, 96, 98–103
Rastenburg 55
Revolt Against the Modern World
    (Evola) 6, 8, 16, 39, 108
Ride the Tiger (Evola) 6, 16, 47
Revolution of 1848 21, 53, 73

Rexism 27
Richelieu, Cardinal 53
Risorgimento 9, 19, 21, 31, 104, 107
Rohan, Karl Anton 95
Roman 12, 14–15, 33–34, 38, 41,
    48, 52, 65, 94, 99, 101, 104,
    107–108, 118, 120
Rome 6–8, 11–12, 14, 16, 26, 31,
    33, 42, 44, 50–52, 60–61, 70, 93,
    107–108, 118
Royal Academy of Italy 60, 76
Rumania 27
Russia 20–21, 31, 40, 67, 97–98,
    109, 112

S

Salazar, António de Oliveira 27, 80
Salò Republic, see Italian Social
    Republic
School of Fascist Mysticism 87
Second World War 8–9, 55, 69, 81,
    86, 88–89, 98, 107, 109–112
Sicily 20, 54
'Significato e funzione della
    monarchia' (Evola) 50
Skorzeny, Otto 15, 55
Social Honour Court 82
socialism 6, 25, 27, 29, 31, 41, 43,
    59, 62, 80–81, 85–86, 91, 95,
    109, 115, 118
Sombart, Werner 90–91, 103
Soviet Union 86, 98, 111, 113
Spain 55, 80, 82
Sparta 101, 107
Spengler, Oswald 31, 65, 90, 96, 99
squadristi 8, 60, 94
Stalinism 42, 63
States-General 19, 73
Stoicism 88
Sudetenland 42
Sulla, Lucius Cornelius 120

T

Third Estate 19, 23, 67
Third Reich 42, 56, 69, 73, 81–82,
    102, 110, 112
totalitarianism 41–42, 45, 48–49,
    77, 82
trade unions 84
Tradition 7, 11, 13–16, 18, 20, 22,
    27, 33, 39, 62, 65, 67–68, 75, 80,
    97, 99, 104, 109, 111, 117, 128
Treaty of Versailles 21
Tripartite Pact (1940) 107–108, 110
Triple Alliance (1882) 20–21
Triple Entente 20–21

U

Udine 62
United Kingdom 2, 20–21
United States of America 7, 11, 15,
    46, 94, 98

V

Vatican 8, 12–15, 33, 38, 63, 99
Verona Manifesto 83–84
Vittorio Emanuele III 53–54, 56

W

West Germany, see Federal Republic
    of Germany
'What the Falange Wants' (Primo de
    Rivera) 67
Wilhelm II 53
World War I, see First World War
World War II, see Second World War

Y

Years of Lead 79

Other books published by Arktos:

Beyond Human Rights
by Alain de Benoist

Manifesto for a European Renaissance
by Alain de Benoist & Charles Champetier

The Problem of Democracy
by Alain de Benoist

Germany's Third Empire
by Arthur Moeller van den Bruck

The Arctic Home in the Vedas
by Bal Gangadhar Tilak

Revolution from Above
by Kerry Bolton

The Fourth Political Theory
by Alexander Dugin

Metaphysics of War
by Julius Evola

The Path of Cinnabar
by Julius Evola

Archeofuturism
by Guillaume Faye

Convergence of Catastrophes
by Guillaume Faye

Why We Fight
by Guillaume Faye

The WASP Question
by Andrew Fraser

War and Democracy
by Paul Gottfried

The Saga of the Aryan Race
by Porus Homi Havewala

Homo Maximus
by Lars Holger Holm

The Owls of Afrasiab
by Lars Holger Holm

De Naturae Natura
by Alexander Jacob

Fighting for the Essence
by Pierre Krebs

Can Life Prevail?
by Pentti Linkola

Guillaume Faye and the Battle of Europe
by Michael O'Meara

The Ten Commandments of Propaganda
by Brian Anse Patrick

A Handbook of Traditional Living
by Raido

The Agni and the Ecstasy
by Steven J. Rosen

The Jedi in the Lotus
by Steven J. Rosen

It Cannot Be Stormed
by Ernst von Salomon

Tradition & Revolution
by Troy Southgate

Against Democracy and Equality
by Tomislav Sunic

The Initiate: Journal of Traditional Studies
by David J. Wingfield (ed.)

Lightning Source UK Ltd.
Milton Keynes UK
UKOW01f0017160716

278526UK00004BA/201/P